For
Heather
Neville

Enjoy!

Brian
Coventry
:)

Aug 2012.

Adopted at Age Four

BRIAN L. COVENTRY

AuthorHouse™
1663 Liberty Drive
Bloomington, IN 47403
www.authorhouse.com
Phone: 1-800-839-8640

This book is a work of fiction. People, places, events, and situations are the product of the author's imagination. Any resemblance to actual persons, living or dead, or historical events, is purely coincidental.

© 2010 Brian L. Coventry. All rights reserved.

No part of this book may be reproduced, stored in a retrieval system, or transmitted by any means without the written permission of the author.

First published by AuthorHouse 8/24/2010

ISBN: 978-1-4520-3614-4 (sc)
ISBN: 978-1-4520-3615-1 (hc)
ISBN: 978-1-4520-3616-8 (e)

Library of Congress Control Number: 2010910964

Printed in the United States of America

This book is printed on acid-free paper.

To Barbara Ann Coventry and Ian Francis James Coventry
My two most favourite persons in my life.

*"Two roads diverged in a wood and I-
I took the one less traveled' by,
And that has made all the difference.*

Robert Frost from a "A Road Not Taken"

Chapter 1.

"Little Leslie, the early years…"

My first remembrances of the orphanage was a very large room with many beds and lots of kids my age in individual beds in a dormitory. The orphanage was located at the corner of Rideau Street and Charlotte in downtown Ottawa. It was operated by the "Children's Aid Society of Ottawa-Hull".

I was a ward of this Agency being given up by my birth mother the day I was born. I had been in foster homes now for 4 years. Nowadays I have no remembrance of those foster homes except that I always ended up back at the residence at Rideau Street and Charlotte, usually in worst condition then when I left.

Back then between 1945 and 1949 there was no welfare it was post-war Canada and foster homes were a source of revenue akin to welfare. Many took in the children accepted the cheques and did the least for these wards.

I was a typical example of this. By the time the Swartmanns came for their first pre-adoption visit I was a wreck. I was underweight for my age, was anemic due to very poor nutrition and wasn't the greatest candidate for adoption at age four.

I still remember sitting on the floor in an interview room and I was playing with some trucks and toys they had given me to distract me from the social worker/prospective adoptive parents conversation which I probably wouldn't have understood in any event.

At the time I didn't realize it but I was the ideal candidate for adoption. Jean Swartmann had had three successive miscarriages and her Doctors explained she was unable to bear children. On top of this problem she was told that her husband's Frank's mother Mrs. Edwina Swartmann was in ill health and looking for one of the family to take her in on a permanent basis.

Mrs. Edwina Swartmann was an old hateful mother-in-law that had given her daughter-in-law Jean a hard time from day one. She had a vile tongue and a mean temper all her life.

So with this in mind and realizing she was barren, the decision to adopt was a simple choice. Put a kid in the upstairs bedroom, no room for Mother-in-law.

Not shortly after I arrived at the Swartmann household as a permanent member, subject to the usual probationary period. This came and went with no hiccups, papers signed, court appearances resolved, name changed legally to Leslie Gerald Swartmann from my original name of Brian Leslie Wallace at birth.

****

From thereon I remember my life clearly.

I used to "act up" because I guess I thought these people would be no better than the ugly foster homes I'd been in before. I guess I thought it's just a matter of time I'd be sent back to the orphanage anyway.

One time I decided to freak them out and I hid in the well of their desk and pulled the chair in so they couldn't find me. I thought I was being smart or cunning but both my then new Mom and Dad freaked out. They ran through the house searching for me, culled the apartment building we lived in, even called the police.

At some point Children's Aid and the Ottawa City Police were informed there was a problem and arrived on the scene. I guess at this point I figured the "jig was up" and I exited my hiding place. The cops weren't too impressed, the Children's Aid worker wasn't too impressed but my new Mom and Dad all they could do was hug me and my Mom Jeanne cried, my Dad Frank smiled and they both told me they loved me and don't ever do that to them again.

It was then I realized I was anchored, not going back to the orphanage and I settled down and started to enjoy my new life. My new Mom figured out I must be enjoying my new home as pretty soon I started to hum and sing around the house. She and my father encouraged my singing and I used to go around our neighbourhood singing for the neighbours. A very popular song of the day was **"There's a Bluebird on my window sill"**. I memorized this song and would sing it to our neighbours with the result that I would receive a candy or a penny or nickel for my efforts. These then were my first "paid" performances.

Although I was settled in I was still pretty rambunctious and I was testing the Swartmann's patience to the limits. I got myself in to trouble of some kind or another on a regular basis. The terrible two's were replaced by the terrible four's. My new mother was trying hard to be patient but every now and then she'd scold me and end up with her famous words; **"Just wait till your Daddy comes home, he'll straighten you out!"**

I don't think my father was all that keen on the role my mother had assigned him as disciplinarian but he would deal out my spankings on the bum with such gems as **" Spare the rod and spoil the child!"** or the best one of all was: **"This hurts me a lot more than it hurts you"**.

When I still acted up in spite of the spankings, he then decided I needed something more attention getting. His friend Mitch Kowalski was the Superintendent in one of the other buildings, a retired military cop and a huge 6 foot 2 inch man. He gave my father one of his old police belts. No longer was it the bare hand spanking the bare ass. It was this huge police belt doubled over and wacked on my buttocks right through my pants.

When he said: **This hurts me more than it hurts you!"** I'd say: **" I don't think so, Poppa!"**

My behaviour improved somewhat after that but never enough to warrant a pat on the back.

****

Looking back now, I think I must have been still in Diapers when I arrived at my new home. They say boys are harder to potty train than girls and I was no exception. My late introduction to the toilet was probably due to the total lack of interest in my development during my many brief assignments to Foster care.

My Dad was assigned that duty by my Mom. He would take me upstairs to the bathroom whenever I decided that the time was fast approaching. He would sit me on the toilet seat and tell me this story that I was a WW2 B52 bomber flying into enemy territory from England. When I was ready I should shout the words: **"BOMBS AWAY!!"**

This proved to be a very effective learning tool as I was always prepared to bomb Hitler and the Nazi's with all I had in the Bombay!

I learned early in life, that stealing wasn't a good thing. One day my Mom and I were up in the boss's big house and I wandered off into a spare bedroom. I was looking in the drawers besides the bed and saw a small battery operated pen-light. I decided this should be mine and stuffed in my pocket. A few day's later my father's boss noticed it was missing. One and one equaled two and they found the penlight in my dresser under some clothes. Did I get a tuning up for that one. Belt and all.

I finally learned my lesson one day after school. I still thought I could pull theft off (Age 5) and I was in a store that was then at the Intersection of Wellington and Albert Street. Where these streets intersected was a triangle and the store was actually constructed as a Triangular building. It was a convenience store. I went in to buy a bubble gum and thought the owner wasn't looking as I headed for the door. I grabbed a Banana off the fruit section and stuffed it into my shirt. The owner said: **"Just one minute, young man, I saw that!"**

He then said:" **"Don't move young lad you're in big trouble."** I froze. Then he placed a call to the Ottawa City Police and before you knew it a Black and White pulled up to the front door of the store. Back then I was being taught the difference between right and wrong. No one was infringing on my "Human Rights" as that was not an issue back then. They only wanted to make sure that I understood that stealing was a crime.

The cop had a discussion with the store owner. I surrendered the banana, and was driven home in the squad car. When I got home I got the third degree from Mom and Poppa.

Needless to say, I learned my lesson and never in the future stole a single thing for the rest of my life and had no use for thieves.

Back in the early fifties the Ottawa Dairy delivered your milk by horse drawn Dairy delivery wagons. The horse Barn for the Ottawa Dairy was close to our apartment building on Empress Street. I can still remember the horse drawn Dairy Wagons coming down the hill at Bronson and Laurier. It was a steep hill and I was impressed with how the driver held back the horses and braked his carriage so the animals wouldn't be injured on that sharp incline.

They came into my backyard and the delivery man came up the backstairs into our building dropping off fresh milk (and cream) in bottles and butter on every doorstep that were customers. On the way out he would collect the empty bottles that his customers had put out the night before.

I used to go around to the Horsebarn on Empress Street to see the horses. Sometimes a good-natured caretaker would let me in to pat the horses on the head and give them a treat. Other times I was told by less accommodating employees: **"Get out of here, kids aren't allowed around the horses! Get lost!"**

****

At school my teachers soon learned in the early grades that I was an avid reader.

I was always the first student up to pick up a book for a reading assignment. I had great English teachers at Wellington Street Public School. One of them introduced me to the Poetry of William Henry Drummond a late 19th century early 20th Century Canadian poet who characterized the French population with their thick accents when they spoke English. I would read these poems and laugh out loud. They were so funny, but I could identify with them as there was a small population of French kids that attended our school from Lebreton Flats. My favorite of them all was: "Little Bateese!"

Little Bateese

You bad leetle boy, not moche you care How busy you're kipin' your poor gran'-pere. Tryin' to stop you ev'ry day Chasin' de hen aroun' de hay--W'y don't you geev' dem a chance to lay? Leetle Bateese!

Off on de feeld you foller der plow, when you get tirer you sick de cow,
Make them scare so dey jump de wall , den der milk ain't good for notting at all!
And yer only five and a half dis fall!! Little Bateese!

There were many other great poems by this author like "De Stove Pipe Hole" and many others but I loved Little Bateese the most because it reminded me of myself, "Leetle Leslee".

My teachers saw my passion for reading and I was encouraged to get up in class and read a chapter of the book of the day. I loved that assignment. Certain kids thought I was trying to be "teacher's pet" or a "suckhole."

I would get reminded of this in the halls and when fight ensued I was the one who always seemed to end up in the Principle's office. Back then you're bad behaviour (fights in the halls) was rewarded with the strap. The Principle was the only one who was allowed to administer this corporal punishment. He would make a big production of it, first a big speech about how the student had erred and there was necessary "correctional measures" required.

Then he'd reach into the drawer in his desk. This was when you were supposed to bust out in tears and repent. If you were from upper Primrose Street or an affluent family you were allowed to break down and forgiveness was forthcoming.

But us badasses from my neighbourhood weren't operating on the same set of rules. We were from poor families who wouldn't argue with the Principle or the School Board. So when we got the strap, we would never show the slightest sign of emotion whatsoever. I took my punishment and never flinched no matter how much it hurt. To do so would be in betrayal of the "Code of the Flats".

But as soon as I exited the Principle's office I was allowed to bust out in tears while I ran all the way to the washroom and make myself look perfectly normal as I sauntered back into my classroom.

****

My grandmother Edwina Swartmann was installed in a Senior Citizen's Home out on Pleasant Park Drive. She complained about the place constantly, every time we went to visit her about once a week. My Dad paid for her rent there over and above what she could afford, even though he couldn't afford it. My Uncle George (My dad's brother, nice job in the Civil Service never volunteered to assist financially.) Yet whenever we visited Grandma Edwina all she ever did was rag on my Dad and praise up Uncle George as he was the best son she ever had and my Dad was a loser.

My Uncle George became my least favourite relative of all. At one time he decided to hang the nickname on me of "Stinky". This was really hurtful and I hated everytime he showed up at our place and shouted out this awful name.

One day my Dad and I were down at Holtz's store on Elgin Street and in walked Uncle George. As soon as he saw me he said: **"Hi Little Stinky!!"**

I started to cry and ran from the store. This was about a dozen city blocks and I walked all the way home by myself in tears. When I got home my Mom asked what was wrong. I told her what had happened at Mr. Holtz's store and she got very angry.

When Dad got home she tuned him up and said: **"Tell that jerk of a brother of yours to lay off with that stupid nickname that he has for Leslie or the next time he shows up here I'll show him my cast iron skillet!"**

The only time my Uncle George did anything for us was when he took us to his cottage on a lake near Kingston. We were to go fishing. As we went around the lake he pointed out a Black Snake Nest in the corner of the lake. There was a big Black snake and it seemed like 20 or 30 baby snakes all swirling around in the edge of the lake. I was very scared by this and used to have nightmares about this afterwards.

We never went back to there again. But Dad and I kept on fishing.

My Dad could make his own lures. He carved small wood dowels and shaped them like minnows. Then he'd paint them with spots and the right colours to make them look like the real thing. He'd install a set of treble hooks and then put a coat of shellac over the finished product to preserve the colour.

One day we were up in Pakenham fishing off the shore below the bridge and he caught a 27 pound Muskie with his homemade lure. It took him about half an hour to get it into shore, but he was very proud of his catch. I was very proud of my Dad and mentally vowed someday I'll catch a fish like that too!

Meanwhile about a week later there was a story in the Ottawa Citizen about some 10 year old kid that had caught a 110 pound Sturgeon in the rapids at Deshenes, Quebec (just outside Aylmer).

I became hooked on fishing for life.

My Mom was an amazing cook as were all her sisters. German decent raised in a German settlement in Eastern Ontario next to Renfrew County. It wasn't long before she fattened me up and sent me off to pre-school kindergarten at Wellington Street Public School that nowadays serves as a parking lot for Government employees. Mom was great at cooking everything but she hated to bake. So once a week she would go down to the "National System of Baking" a bakery store located on Bank Street between Laurier Avenue and Slater Street. There she would buy sugar cookies, pies and my favourites: shortbread cookies with walnuts imbedded in the tops. They were very dry but tasted fantastic with a glass of milk. She also got Chelsea Buns for my Dad: his favourite.

****

I found out early in life about discrimination. Here I was in a neighborhood mostly composed of Irish, English and Italian settlers and their offsprings. I had a much darker completion than anyone in the school and so I was subjected to taunts like: **"Are you part nigger?"** or **"are you a Chink?"** So I'd go home and ask my Mom **"What's a nigger? What's a Chink?"** My mom said to me **"Look in the mirror son and what do you see?** I said:**" I see me."** Mom said:**" You know what you are? You're a Canadian, that's all, a little darker complexion than those kids at school but you're every bit as good as them, probably better because you don't say the hateful things they are saying to you."**

Half way through the year a new girl arrived in our class. She was Polish and her name was Inga Kwasniewski. She had a dark complexion like me but had a beautiful face that to me looked like Debbie Reynolds, 8 year old version. I fell instantly in to (puppy) love with her.

Meanwhile, at school the same bunch that had tormented me decided to pick on her. One day the jerk from upper Primrose Street asked her in a loud voice so everyone could hear: **"Hey Inga, you know why Polish names all end in "ski?"**

Inga replied: **"No, why?"**

The jerk said: **"'Cause they can't spell toboggan!!"**

His audience all had a great guffaw at that one.

I thought to myself: (You asshole, picking on a new kid like that. Where are your brains?)

I saw tears fill up in Inga's eyes and she ran from the school yard to her house which was across the street from the school. She didn't return that day, but was back the next day.

As she was walking down the hall she met the jerk from Upper Primrose Street and as she passed him she spat out the words **"Swinia! Palant!"** at him.

The Jerk said: **"What did you say?"** and Inga came back with: **"If you're so smart, figure it out yourself!"**

I asked her later what that meant and she said: **"It told him he was a jerk and a bastard in Polish."**

After that Inga and I became childhood sweethearts but this was soon to end. Her father got transferred out to British Columbia with his job and Inga vanished after one Friday afternoon, never to return.

****

Back at home at the Swartmann's…

We didn't have a television, but we had a radio and a record player. Every noon I listened to our local radio station CFRA that aired "North Star Roundup". I grew up on Eddie Arnold, Hank Williams Sr. and the Sons of the Pioneers". Frank Ryan gave the "Farmer's Notebook" In that hour as well as well. All the farmer's in the Ottawa Valley and Eastern Ontario tuned in to him to here the latest cattle and farm commodity prices updated daily.

At night, my Mom would put on some 78 rpm records which could include the likes of Perry Como, The Andrews Sisters, Theresa Brewer or Nelson Eddy signing duet with Jeanette McDonald She loved the Big Band orchestras like Glen Miller and Duke Ellington. . She also played Enrico Caruso, her favourite. Music became a major part of my life from the day I set foot in our home.

One of Nelson Eddy's songs that really stuck with me was about the Mounties: The Royal Canadian Mounted Police. His song went something like this:

"Up o'er the trails, like pack of angry wolves on the trail,
We are out to get you, **dead or alive,**
We are out to get you dead or alive,
Better get away,
If you're the one,
Better run, put your gun away,
If you're the one, better run, better run away,
Here come the Mounties to get the man they're after now!"

I became fascinated with the RCMP and decided that's what I wanted to be when I grew up, an RCMP officer.

Every Christmas, I was allowed to stay up to listen to "Letters to Santa" on CFRA. Whoever was doing Santa sure had me convinced especially when he'd say his famous line: **"Bless my buttons!!!"**. Only the real Santa could come out with a line like that!

I wrote my letters to Santa. After I looked in the Simpson's Sears catalogue I knew what I wanted. There was two things near and dear to my heart. First, #1 on my list to Santa: In the Simpson's Sears catalogue there's a Mountie outfit with the redcoat and the striped pants and black boots. That's my #1 choice Santa. If you don't have any left, I'd like the cowboy outfit with the cowboy hat, six guns with the holsters and the cowboy boots…

This was not to be. The Swartmanns couldn't afford such things and I ended up with a sailor's oufit, much more practical and affordable for my parents.

Back then I remember I required speech therapy. I believe it had something to do with both my malnutrition and abuse in the foster homes. I had a major problem with "the" and "s" sounds and I stuttered. In time it was corrected, but to this day sixty years later, if I'm tired or stressed I can have the odd lapse on an "s" or a "the". The school administration set me up with the speech therapist in Junior Kindergarten (you were allowed to enroll at age 5) back then there was Junior Kindergarten and Senior Kindergarten and then Grade one.

There was the school Superintendent, "Mr.Powell". He mostly hung around the Boiler room and always had a scowl on his face. All the kids in the school were afraid of him. He liked it that way as he didn't want any students coming into his private place, the boiler room. I was scared of him too, but I didn't realize he was good friends with my Dad who was the Superintendent at the Apartment Building across the street from my school. I didn't realize it then but looking back I realize he cut me more slack than the rest of the kids and was even somewhat protective of me. He was also a WW2 veteran. One day I came in to the Furnace Room and heard him humming a tune I recognized from "Snow White and the

Seven Dwarfs" . It was "whistle while you work". I said to Mr. Powell "I know that song: It's from a Walt Disney Movie!" He said**:" No sonny. Back in World War 2 when we soldiers were marching from one position to another or when we were laying in the ditches waiting for enemy fire or returning it we used to sing a different version of that song."** He then sang me the following:

Whistle while you work, Hitler is a jerk, Mussolini bit his weenie, now it doesn't work!

He ended off by saying that song used to drive the Germans and Italians crazy. At the time I didn't clue into the significance of the lyrics but later on I got it.

Back then arithmetic was a complete different story than today. No calculators, just a piece of paper and a pencil and arithmetic problems to solve using your brains. I enjoyed arithmetic in the lower grades. Addition, subtraction, multiplication, division. Even then you'd get a combination of questions where you would have to mix up a combination of division and addition and then fractions to get the final answer. I loved that. But later in High School : Algebra and Geometry. I hated it with a passion. Who cares whether $x+y=z$? I couldn't care less.

Back then there was a street that was halfway between Commissioner and Booth on the North side of Albert Street. It is no longer there being eliminated in favour of a Government Employee parking lot. But a the corner of this street was a grocery store and next door was a large tenement apartment, shabby, rundown housing poor families, on the edge of Lebreton Flats.

One of the families were the Wilsons. There was a mother and father and five children ranging from newborn to early teen. My schoolmate was eight years old named Barry.

One fateful night their building caught on fire. There were no fire codes enforced in those days and the fire spread through the building like wildfire. By the time the Fire Department arrived the building was engulfed in flames. Everyone got out except one. The Wilson's did a head count and realized that Lisa, Barry's younger four year old sister hadn't made it. Barry was frantic. He told the fireman his sister was still in there but they told him it's too late the building is unsafe nobody can go back in.

He wouldn't listen to them. Before they could stop him he ran straight into the building and disappeared. He ran into the building and located Lisa laying on the floor in their ground floor living room. She had started to follow everyone else, tripped and fell on the floor, knocking herself out momentarily. By the time Barry reached her she was coming to and coughing from the smoke. He grabbed her, threw her over his shoulders and charged out of the building just as the rear started to crumble near collapse. He came charging out of the building and about ten feet out collapsed from sheer exhaustion and smoke inhalation. But both survived. Barry was an instant hero. And well deserving of it. I'll bet Lisa has lots to say about Barry to her children and grandchildren these days……

There was one boy in about Grade 5 that was a bit of a problem. He was always hitting on the pretty girls and if they didn't appreciate his advances he targeted them for punishment. It started out as a trip or a slap from behind in the aisles between classes. Then one day he brought a 12 inch ruler to school with a nail driven through the end. He was going up and down the halls smacking these girls that had rejected him with the ruler and drawing blood with each smack. I noticed him after about the forth smack and I snuck up behind him and grabbed his weapon then proceeded to smack him everywhere I could hit him until a teacher restrained me and took away the infamous ruler. For my indiscretion I received the Strap from the principle. But I was a hero to those girls.

There was a Municipal Swimming Pool just below Wellington Street on Booth Street. In the summer of my eighth year they shut this pool down permanently because many of the local kids were suffering from some form of skin infection. I wasn't spared. My Mom took me to the Doctor and he told her I had a rare form of polio. It was hard to treat but I was given medicine. The medicine didn't work. My skin rashes got worst. My Mom & Dad heard about this lady who was a faith healer in the Anglican Ministry. She happened to be coming to Ottawa so my Mom and Dad put me on her list of potential candidates for faith healing.

I remember going up to Christ Church Cathedral in a small office where this lady received us. After some conversation, she put both hands on my head and started to pray to God. This went on for a long time and then we left. Within a week, my scabs and skin discoloration were gone. My Mom took me back to our Doctor who was amazed at my recovery. His parting words as we left were

"There are many things on earth that can't be explained by science or medicine".

Chapter 2.

But life goes on.

My father was the most honest man I ever met in my entire life. He never swore, would never tell a lie, didn't smoke, didn't drink alcohol of any kind and attended church religiously. He had little education (Maybe Grade 3) was sent out to work at age 6 in Kingston (being born in 1903, that wasn't unusual) . He told me he delivered papers and picked up the garbage at the back of Restaurants and hauled it away to the dumps for a few cents per job.

I never once heard him utter a curse. He had his own sanitized profanities (if you could call them that). Such as "Goll-darn" or "Gosh-Darn". The best one that left everyone scratching their heads was " Gosh All Fish-hooks!" You couldn't help but love the guy.

One of my favourite expressions of his was when he noticed someone driving erratically ahead of him he'd say: **"That guy is all over the road like a dose of salts!!"**

Another one of his gems was if some motorist passed him really fast, he'd say: **"Where's the fire, Mack?"** As they passed by…Every other motorist was Mack.

He was bound and determined he would raise me as a good Anglican boy during every step of the way.

First, he enrolled me as an alter boy at about age 6. If one were to go into the CBC archives I guess one could find a Church Service at Christ Church Cathedral when I was the cross bearer at that age in a televised service, maybe 4 feet tall in a red and white cassock bearing the cross in front of the alterboys and celebrants of that particular service. I remember we all had to have make-up on our faces (powder & rouge to make us look good on television due to lighting issues with the camera equipment in those days)

As I got older I was enlisted in the Junior Choir at Christ Church Cathedral, I had a good voice as a young soprano and Godfrey Hewitt was the celebrated organist and choirmaster of this Church encouraged me at choir practices to learn the tough stuff. He told me **"you can be Head Singer in the Senior Choir someday if you apply yourself, Leslie!"**

It was in the choir I first received an appreciation of classical music. A lot of our music was from the great classical composers. I then started to listen more carefully to the works of these great artists. I became particularly partial to Handel, Tchaikovsky, Beethoven and Mozart.

I loved Swan Lake, the Dance of the Sugar Plum Fairy by Tchaikovsky and Morning by Handel.

Along about that time there was a flutist in Toronto named Moe Kauffman. He made a recording that went to number one on the hit parade called "Swinging Shepherd Blues". At some point I learned to whistle this song as if I were the flute. One night I whistled it for the guys in the choir. Godfrey Hewitt heard me in the hallway and exclaimed: **"Swartmann, when you whistle like that you have perfect pitch! Work on that voice of yours the same way!"**

I was still thinking forward to the day that I might just make it to Head Soloist of the Senior choir but this was never to be. Later on just before I turned thirteen I came down with bout of pleurisy that saw me bedridden for the whole month of March. When I finally recovered, my voice had changed it was now cracking somewhere between a preteen boy's voice and male adult voice. My singing days were over for a year or two until my voice fully changed over.

Back at Junior Choir. One day after practice, I was about 6 or 7 all the choir boys were allowed to go play up in Lauder Hall (a large meeting room upstairs in the back of the church used for special meetings, church bazaars etc.) It was always empty after choir practices.

That time we were all playing cowboys and Indians. In the heat of the fracas someone tipped over a big radiator heater which fell directly on my ankle, making a compound fracture. This required a cast, crutches and limping for some months thereafter.

I might mention this happened to my left foot. Everything always happens to my left foot.

Years before this my Dad had to pick up a parcel at Union Station. Anyone familiar with the history of Ottawa would know that this was across from what is now the Rideau Centre/ Congress Centre and approximately where the Westin Hotel is located. The Train Station was located there as well as the train tracks besides the Rideau Canal.

My Dad took me down with him to pick up some parcel and left me in the warehouse adjacent to the parcel pick-up room for seconds. That's all I needed. At age 5 you don't have a clue about risks or danger. All I knew was there was a box of cheeping baby chicks on the top of a huge tractor rim. Of course, I decided to climb that tractor rim to investigate those cheeping chicks.

The next thing I remember is waking up in the Ottawa Civic Hospital in a room full of Doctors and Nurses working on (you guessed it) my left foot.

Apparently, the Tractor rim lost balance when I started to climb it, I was thrown away from its fall but the edge of it landed on my left foot, crushing all my toes and toe-nails. They had to surgically remove all my toe-nails (what was left of them) set all my toes in casts and hope for the best. Anyway the toe-nails grew back in, the toes set well but as I went through life I never have had a problem with my right foot, it's like my left foot is jinxed.

****

Back then I was a bit of an explorer. I used to take off from my place and sometimes I'd end up at my Uncle's place on Isabella Street on the other side of the railroad tracks (now they call it the Queensway!)

There was an article in The Ottawa Citizen that went like this:

"Five year old boy caught crossing against the Red Light at Gladstone and Bank Street".

The Ottawa Police brought me home in a squad car and after that Mom and Dad used to put a leather harness on me with a long rope tied to the steel fence in our backyard. That way I only had a certain radius to move in and they could keep an eye on me from their apartment. This went on for that summer but I was unshackled in my 6th year.

My Dad never called me by my name but my Mom always referred to me as Leslie. From the beginning when I settled down and felt comfortable in my new adoptive home I called my new mother Mom and my new father "Poppa".

He always referred to me as "Sonny Boy". That never bothered me, I kind of liked it and never wondered why he didn't use my given name. As I grew older "Sonny Boy" became "Sonny" and for my part "Poppa" became "Pop". He remained "Pop" until the day he died.

In one of my year five year old expeditions I ended up walking down the railroad tracks that ran beside the Rideau Canal by Union Station and found a half-dead pigeon that had been hit by a train. It's wing was broken and it was bleeding. I picked it up and held it close to my chest and calmed it down as it resisted me a bit at first. Then I walked it home (about 12 blocks). It bled a lot on my jacket but by the time I got home with my Mom went into nurse mode and stopped the bleeding, put a splint and make shift cast on the broken wing. I named the pigeon "Goo Goo" because that what she said constantly. She had a new home in a cardboard box in the kitchen.

After a few weeks of constant feeding and watering Goo Goo regained her strength and started testing her healed wing. Mom took off the cast and let her try her flapping unrestrained. She was better. My Mom said you realize she's not a pet and you'll have to let her go now and go back to her kind, Leslie. She said take her outside now and see if she's well enough to return to Nature.

I took Goo Goo out in the back yard and held her in my hands not really wanting to let her go. Eventually I opened my cupped hands and said: **" Go Goo Goo, go!!"**

When she realized I had let her go, she flapped her wings a couple of times, then stood up on her feet and flew out of my hands. She flew well and went in ever increasing circles around the backyard, eventually flying away for good. I said**:" Goodbye, Goo Goo!!"**

****

My Dad was a Property Manager of 4 different properties in Ottawa. He with limited education took care of 4 Apartment Building complexes ranging from a 12 Unit on Cambridge Street, a 18 Unit on Albert Street, a 15 unit on Gloucester Street and a 6 unit on Gladstone Ave. He was a bargain for his employer because he was willing at first to accept $150 per month plus a 2 Bedroom Apartment which later (out of the goodness of her heart) she decided this should be boosted to $200 per month plus the apartment. If you consider the fact that he was on call 24/7 sometimes worked Saturdays and Sundays fixing this and that he was being paid at ridiculous low wages, only because he was too easy going and thought he had the best deal out there.

My mother collected all the rents and interviewed prospective tenants filling in rent applications which were passed on the Landord for Approval. She received no compensation for this. This was part of the $200 per month plus apartment deal.

The only other thing his employer threw in as a "perk" was each summer for about 4 years from when I was 6 years old until 10, she would enroll me in and fund the cost of my 2 week attendance at a kid's summer camp. This always a religious based facility where there was lots of praying, hymn singing and Bible studying (between outdoor activities).

At the summer camp outside of Manotick in the first year of these paid summer camps I inherited the name of "Bugjuice". This was because they served gallons of Kool-Aid and I drank as much as I could get my hands on. That was the term everyone used for this particular super-cheap beverage.

The following year I was sent to the "Christian Bible Camp" in Kemptville.

I was age 9 by now and I had taken up a friendship with of all people my father's boss's nephew. We decided we were going to tree climb. We chose a Red Pine. (It's like a ladder the way the braches spiral out) Anyway we started to climb and up we went. About half way up my buddy stepped on the wrong rotten branch and down he went hitting multiple bruising, ripping branches on the way down many feet from the initial plunge. We had to get an ambulance and he survived after multiple stitches and surgery. Needless to say, my Dad's Boss wasn't to impressed. After age 10, I opted out from these summer camps with a "Thanks but no thanks."

I was indoctrinated into the work ethic at an early age. I saw how hard my Dad worked and when asked to help (encouraged by a $1.00 per week allowance) I chipped in. This could be in the form of picking up the garbage set outside the 12 apartments in our particular building and hauling this down to "the garbage room" in a big warehouse in the backyard of this complex. Or I was asked the polish the brass number sign on the front door of the apartment building as well as the brass letter boxes inside the front door and the brass door knob at the entrance door.

When my father was sick with the flu or a bad cold, I did the garbage run every day until he was back on his feet. By the time I was ten years old, I also took on the task of sweeping all the halls of the 12 unit building and once a week I washed down all those halls with a mop and pail full of hot water laced with Industrial strength cleaner, followed by dry mopping the entire halls. Back then it seemed like there was about 5 miles of hallways....

All these properties owned by my father's employers were buildings with "furnished apartments" Therefore he also managed three warehouses of furniture from beds, mattresses, hideabeds, stoves, fridges, coffee tables dining room tables, kitchen dinettes, etc. Later on as I got older, I started to help move furniture.. When I was small it was small stuff (like table lamps and end tables). As I got older it was bigger stuff (like coffee tables and small chairs and stools and ottomans). Into my teens I got into the Heavy lifting: Fridges, stoves, hideabeds, couches, mattresses , even at one point a piano (five men moving it up a circular staircase!). I found out later in life that this basically screwed up my back as when you're a teen your spine is green, still developing and shouldn't be subjected to lifting Simmons Hideabeds or Pianos!!

The only perk I received beyond my allowance was free passes to the Centre Theatre on Sparks Street. This was because my Mom shopped at some grocery store that gave out theatre passes after you bought a certain amount of groceries. Sometimes she got two passes and we would go together. It was those times I was allowed to watch movies like "the Student Prince" or "Casablanca" . I told Mom she was a dead ringer for Ingrid Bergman and she said **"Thanks Leslie"** and I got a big mommy hug.

When I went by myself, I always took the Hardy Arcade that went from Queen Street to Sparks. It had a slanted hallway that went up at a less than 45 degree angle. Near the top there was a left hand hallway that led to the offices of Josef Karsh the prize winning Internationally acclaimed photographer. In the hall besides his office entrance there were some of his pictures in glassed in framed enclosures. His work would always stop you in your tracks.

****

Back then there was a singer named Doris Day. She was beautiful, blonde haired, the American dream girl. She starred in many movies and recorded a lot of songs that did well on the hit parade. One of those songs was "Once I had a secret Love".

Somehow or other I heard that someone had revised the lyrics into a convoluted version of her hit song. Instead of her lyrics they were replaced by this: (If you remember Doris Day's version you'll get this immediately)......

Sung by a guy...

" Once I had a secret love,
She wore a nylon negligee,
When our night of love was through,
She said, I didn't have to pay.
So I asked her why her love was free,
She said, Sealy's Mattress sponsored me,
Last night we were on Channel Four,
And my secret love's no secret anymore..."

By the time I was thirteen I was also recruited for the painting jobs. But now I was getting $1.00 an hour. My Dad and I painted apartments after a tenant moved out, we painted hallways in the four apartment complexes, we sanded hardwood floors and refinished them in Stain and varnish. One summer, we painted all the halls of the 18 Unit on Albert Street even in insufferable heat because it had to be done.

There was a Dairy on Somerset Street near Bank Street where we worked close by and my Dad would take me there at the end of a hot Day's work and buy me a great big milk shake. After you finished a huge glass of this, the lady at the counter would bring over what was left in the mixer and empty it into the glass.

This was the year I bought my first ever brand new piece of clothing.

I had just got paid my last week's pay in August before school started, $40.00 cash. I convinced my Dad to drive me out to Towers Department

Store on Cyrville Road. I bought a red white and blue nylon windbreaker and had change left over. I was as proud as a peacock wearing that new jacket. My mother finally convinced me days later to take it off so she could wash it.

Up until then the only new clothes I ever got was at Christmas from my father's boss. Everything else I wore was either purchased at the Ottawa Neighbourhood Services "nearly new" store or were hand me downs from my cousins in Hardwood Lake and Kingston.

Chapter 3.

But we've fast forwarded to age 13. Let's go back again to the early years.

Soon after my adoption I was acquainted with my new extended family. First on my mother's side, she had a two sisters in Ottawa. There was two younger sisters Mary and Paula. Mary was married to a Federal Government employee. She had struck paydirt as he made good wages and they were quite comfortable living in a upper scale home close to the Rideau Canal off of Elgin Street. Mary was the snob of the family. She had two children a girl Andrea and a younger son Harold.

My Aunt Paula was a different story. She worked as a housekeeper in Rockliffe park for a very affluent family as their cook, housekeeper and Governess. She had been married and had one child, a boy she named Trevor. Her husband had tried to kill her in a faked accident shortly after she gave birth to her son, but she managed to escape unharmed and the husband disappeared never to return. So she took the job in Rockliffe to make ends meet, but relied a lot on her sister Mary to take care of young Trevor during the lean years. So Trevor actually grew up with Aunt Mary and cousins Andrea and Harold.

I recall one day my Mom was visiting her sister Mary. I was left alone with my new cousins Andrea, Harold and Trevor. Somehow the conversation turned to how I was their new cousin and I was informed **"You're not our real relative, 'cause you're not a blood relative: YOU'RE ADOPTED. You're not real family!"**

That cut like a knife and I thought to myself I hope this is not what all my new relatives are like!

I was very happy when my Mom said it was time to go home.

Then I got a taste of the better side of my extended family. First my Aunt Georgina up in Hyndford Ontario. She and my Uncle Joseph had a 100 acre farm that bordered on the Madawaska River. They raised beef cattle, pigs and chickens for the eggs. They farmed with 2 teams of Clydesdale horses.

The first time I arrived in our old car (as I recall it was an old Model T Ford) my Uncle Joe said your Aunt Georgina was either in the henhouse or the barn. So my Mom said **"Go find your Aunt, Leslie!"**

I checked out the Henhouse, nobody there. I checked out the barn, same thing. When I went behind the barn there was my new Aunt Georgina putting a bandage on a calf. As soon as she saw me she said **"You must be my new nephew Leslie!"** and gave me a big Renfrew County hug. I grabbed her hand and dragged her back to the farmhouse where Mom and Dad and Uncle Joe were waiting and I said **"Look who I found!!!"**

As if that wasn't great after my less inspiring cousins in Ottawa, I had another great experience the very next day.

Mom and Dad now took me up to Denbigh to introduce me to my Grandma Hannah and my other Aunt Beatrice. But that was just the start.

Later in the day along came my other relatives, the Neumans. There was my Aunt Jessie (Mom's youngest sister) her husband Jethro and their children (my cousins) three boys Virgil, Jessie and Timmy and two girls Kathleen and Mildred (all in descending order).

The first thing I noticed was Aunt Jessie grabbed me and gave me a big Lennox and Addington hug. Uncle Jethro gave me a big smile and shook my hand. Then I was swarmed by my new cousins asking me questions, shaking my hand and making me feel very welcome. We were instantly connected. After that we were allowed to play together, so the boys played cowboys and Indians and fished in the creek below the house. We would catch chubs and brook trout.

My Aunt Beatrice also welcomed me with open arms. She sort of beamed at me and then at my Mom as this part of the family seemed to understand that I was a welcome addition to the family. My Grandma Hannah was already quite old and although she couldn't speak any English (never bothered to learn it) she said many things in German that sounded to me like she was happy I was there and part of the family.

My other cousin Rosie wasn't there on my first visit.

But a month or two later, we made the trip back to visit Grandma and Aunt Beatrice. This time cousin Rosie was there. She was a beautiful teenage girl that had been adopted by Grandma and Aunt Beatrice after she was born out of wedlock by my Aunt Mary. Right after Rosie was born, my Aunt Mary took off to Ottawa, abandoning her baby girl and leaving her to be raised by her mother and Aunt Beatrice.

Rosie and I connected right from the start. We went for walks together, talked about every subject under the sun and became very close.

On the neighbouring farm there was a clearing in the bush with a really big rockface. We'd go there and sit on the rock and talk and talk.

She always had some small gift for me to take back to Ottawa: **"so you'll remember me, Leslie".** Sometimes it was a picture in a small frame. Once it was a transistor radio. But then, when she was 18, she decided to go and be recruited in the female Canadian Naval Corps known as the "Wrens".

I was up there the week before she left for good. She went into her bedroom and came out with this enormous guitar and said: **"I could never learn to play this sucker so it's your's Leslie!"** Meanwhile I was a little runt of a guy and she was a big gal almost six feet tall.

Needless to say, it was the biggest present she had ever given me but later I was too frustrated to try to learn how to play it as my little fingers couldn't get around the neck and learn to play the chords.

Rosie ended up in HMCS Shelbourne Nova Scotia and we became penpals as she started her Naval Career. As the years went by she ended up in Norfolk, Virginia and married a US Naval worker on a US Submarine. After that the letters stopped.

****

I had got along so well with Grandma Hannah and Aunt Beatrice that my Mom decided I could go up there for two weeks of my summer holidays. I was having a ball catching brook trout in the creek below their house and Aunt Beatrice showed me how to clean them and fry them up on the woodstove with flour and butter.

Grandma Hannah was getting quite fragile by now and basically made it from her bed to the couch and the kitchen table. Meanwhile, Aunt Beatrice was teaching me the German Language. I began to notice almost immediately the similarities between Germanic and English. Later in High School, they actually taught this information in the early 60's. We were told that Europe developed into two distinct root languages, the Latin and Gaelic derivatives.

The Latin or Romance language spawned Italian, Spanish, French and Portugese.

Meanwhile, Gaelic to the north spawned German, Dutch, Polish, the Slavics,

And then into Britain Gaelic and English.

As I was learning German from Aunt Beatrice I realized the similarities between German and English. For example: Mother was "Mutter" Mr. was "Herr" the word forbidden was "verboten".

My Aunt Beatrice and I walked the mile from their house to Denbigh once a week for supplies. Those were my German language training sessions.

One night when we were asleep the fox came by and killed Grandma's favourite hen, a Rhode Island Red. She had laid the biggest nicest brown eggs in the whole chicken coop. The next day Grandma was saying things in German I mostly understand and I figured she was pretty upset.

I decided I was going to trap that fox so he wouldn't kill any more of Grandma's chickens. Aunt Beatrice and I on our weekly trip to town rehearsed what I would say to Grandma.

The English version would have went like this:

"**The fox came last night and killed one of your chickens.**

"**Yes Leslie, Your Aunt Beatrice told me, it was my favourite hen too. She laid big brown eggs!**"

Well, Grandma, I'm going to fix that fox. I'm going to build a trap with bait and catch him tonight. Then tomorrow I'll kill him so he won't eat any more of your chickens.

Grandma said: **I think an eight year old boy underestimates the cleverness of a fox.**

We'll see Grandma. I'm going to take a heavy wooden box, put some bloody meat in it, and when the fox grabs the bait, the box will fall on him and trap him.

Grandma Said: **We'll see, Leslie, we'll see…"**

THE NEXT DAY…

"**Well Leslie did you catch that stupid fox?**"

No Grandma, He's not so stupid, he grabbed the bait, sprang the trap and ruined my plan.

Well Leslie, I think the only way you'd stop that fox is with a bullet. And we don't own a gun.

I guess that fox was smarter than I thought.

The German version went like this:

Grossmutter, der fuchs ist letzte nacht gekommen und hat eines unserer huhner getotet..

Ja Leslie, deine tante Beatrice sagte es mir. Es war meine rote lieblings henne. Sie legte grosse braune eier.

Grossmutter, ich werd's dem fuchs beibringen. Ich bau eine falle mit koder und werde ih heute nacht fangen. Dann werde Ich ihn am nachsten tag toten so dass er keine huhner mehr toten kann.

Ich glaube ein acht jahriger junge unterschatzt die schlauheit eines fucases.

Wier werden sehn Grossmutter. Ich werde eine schwere holtzkiste nehmen, etwas blutiges fleisch hinein tuhn und wenn der fuchs den koder nimmt wird die kiste auf ihn fallen und ihn fangen.
Wier werden sehn Leslie, wier werden sehn...

****

Na Leslie, hast du den bloden fuchs gefangen?
Nein, Grossmutter, er ist garnicht so blod. Er hat den koder geschnappt, ohne erwischt zu werden und hat meinen plan ruiniert.
Na Leslie, Ich glaube du kannst den fuchs nur mit einer kugel stoppen, und wir haben kein gewehr.
Ich glaube der fuchs war schlauer als ich dachte.

****

When I was eight years old my Grandma Hannah died leaving my Aunt Beatrice alone in the old house up in Denbigh. Not long after that Aunt Beatrice got very sick and her Doctor in Eganville referred her to the Ottawa Civic hospital where she was diagnosed with severely advanced terminal cancer of the bowels. In those days that was a death sentence. They informed her she might have weeks to live at best. There was no Health Insurance and no real treatment for this cancer in those days so she was sent home to die. My Mom took her in and Mom and Dad gave up their bedroom upstairs and installed a hide-a-bed in the living room which they rolled out every night and slept downstairs.

Aunt Beatrice was given pain killers, but went down rapidly. She lost control a lot and my Mom had to clean up a lot of messes for several weeks before Aunt Beatrice finally passed away. My bedroom was next to hers and I can still remember the stink my Mom had to bear to care for her dying sister.

I told her she was a saint to put up with that. She shrugged and said: **"She's my sister Leslie, you do what you have to do…."**

After Aunt Beatrice died my parents didn't move back up to their bedroom. First they opened all the windows for about a week, closing the door and airing out the room. They got rid of all the bedsheets and the mattress. They disinfected the whole place and washed everything in the room. Afterwards they put in a new mattress, sheets, pillows and bedclothes. My mother had got the idea they should advertise and take in a boarder to help with the budget.

Pretty soon they had a young man installed in the room. He was training to be an RCMP constable out at "N" Division in Rockliffe. He was a very nice fellow originally from Bancroft. He paid $60 per month for his R&B and when he saw the meals my Mom prepared, realized he had got a bargain!

Mom had another brainstorm. She decided to apply to "Dominion Provisioners" from an ad she saw in the newspaper. You signed up for a certain length of time and you got a brand new chest freezer loaded with frozen foods. There was everything supplied: frozen meat, frozen vegetables and fruit. Then there was fish, T.V. Dinners, frozen desserts including pies and frozen juices that you mixed with water.

The whole deal was financed at X dollars per month through Citizen's Finance Company at 28% interest. By the time you got the loan paid off you had no more frozen food but you had a fully paid for freezer!

My Mom was a very proud lady and although she accepted the fact that she was stuck in a low budget lifestyle with not much hope of improvement, she allowed herself and Dad and I one luxury. This took a lot of work on her part. She would scrounge pennies, nickels and dimes. She took on an Avon Franchise and sold cosmetics to friends, relatives, Dad's boss and tenants in the apartment buildings.

Then once per month we'd have to go out for "Mommy's monthly Treat".

This would be a Sunday noon Dinner at an upper scale Ottawa Restaurant. We all had to dress up nicely, Pop in a suit, Mom in her best dress and me in a clean pair of slacks and a white shirt.

Her favourite restaurant was The Green Valley on Prince of Wales Drive beside the Experimental Farm. They had a kid's menu and I always got a nice hot dog or small hamburger, but the main treat was at the end of the meal I got the "Mickey Mouse Ice Cream Platter!" This was a dish with ice cream and whipped cream and pieces of chocolate that looked on the plate like a picture of Mickey Mouse!

Pop liked the Individual Chicken Pot Pie. Whenever he ordered it, he couldn't pronounce "individual" and it would come out: **"I'd like the Invisible Chicken Pot Pie."**

The waitress would smile sweetly and write it down on her order pad. Mom usually ordered "sweetbreads". They looked good but I never tried them until later on and they were delicious made from veal breaded and cooked in vegetable oil and spices.

My Mom scrimped and scraped and every month so she'd have saved enough for this special luxury day. My Dad never objected as he knew how important it was to her to rise above her lot at least once per month.

She had her other favourite spots. There was the Bytown Inn at the corner of Queen and O'Connor (now long gone). And of course the Green Valley.

Once a year at Christmas, they would go to the Chateau Laurier Hotel for the Christmas turkey dinner. This was the biggest expenditure of the year.

Then there was the "Locanda" . This was a restaurant just east of Bank Street on Laurier. It was owned and operated by the parents of Paul Anka who was a teenage heartthrob early Rock and Roll artist, later to become a regular Las Vegas Entertainer. He (Paul) was never there but his parents were absolute gems. They greeted you at the door. They escorted you to your table. They were always on my case that I should join the Boy Scouts. They made my Mom and Dad feel special. I loved the Ankas.

My Dad's boss had an elderly mother in her seventies. The family owned a Packard Clipper which back then was a very upper-scale automobile akin to a Cadillac or a Lincoln. One of my Dad's duties was once a month to take the boss's Mother out to Beechwood Cemetary. She would always have fresh flowers to lay at her late husband's grave. He had one of the biggest most ornate gravestones in the cemetary.

Afterwards, we would take her on a little cruise through Rockliffe and Rockliffe park, the upper crust section of town. This was so she could admire all the mansions on her way back home.

There was a pavilion in the middle of Rockliffe Park. We always stopped there for our major Sunday afternoon treat. Hot dogs, soft drinks and ice cream cones. The boss lady's mother always paid the tab. This was another so called perk for my Dad since he was sacrificing his Sunday afternoon once a month for his employer. Why her daughter couldn't do this for her own mother is still a mystery to me.

****

At about age 10 I started to question my Mom about my birth mother. I realize now she was being protective of me in her own way. But it was all lies. She told me one time she was on very good terms with my birth mother, that they had chats from time to time. Even had tea together so she could update my birthmom on my progress.

At one point she said **"Your birth mother works at that little restaurant at O'Connor Street between Sparks and Wellington'.**

With that information, I went to that Restaurant regularly checking out the female employees that could possibly be the person that would qualify by appearance to be my birth mother. Not a chance. Dead end. One time there was a lady who looked something like me in her features, but I was too chicken to approach her.

One day both Mom and Dad were gone somewhere in the car, so I snooped in their bedroom. My Mom was a great Diary person. There were multiple Diaries in her Dresser. Lo and behold I found one about the time they adopted me. It referred to how much they both wanted me, that they decided to change my name to Leslie Gerald Swartmann from my original name at birth which had been Brian Leslie Wallace. They decided to keep the Leslie and abandon the Brian part.

There were entries from the first time they contacted the Children's Aid to after I was adopted. They went like this:

June 12th, 1949 I contacted the Social worker today at Children's Aid. She said they just received a 3 year old boy, almost four brought back from Foster Care. She said he was run-down but a good home and proper nutrition could fix that. We could meet him tomorrow afternoon at 3:00 p.m.

June 13th, 1949 We finally met Brian. He is very shy and looks sickly. The social worker told us that he's a nice boy but has been sent to Foster Homes where other foster kids pick on him and he also hasn't had a proper diet.

June 20th, 1949 We are allowed to bring Brian home with us for a day to see how it works out. The Social worker came last week to check out our apartment. She seemed impressed with how clean I keep the place but also the religious picture on the wall where Jesus is standing behind a person at the wheel of a ship sort of guiding him. Our Boss gave us that picture. The Crucifix on the wall might have helped too.

June 30th, 1949 We've been accepted to adopt Brian. I am so happy. Frank is very pleased too as he always wanted a son.

Later on in life, I got really frantic to find my roots so I started to comb the Ottawa phone book for Wallaces. I found a lady that ran a dog kennel in Kemptville called "Wallaces Pampered Canines." I phoned her and the conversation went something like this (a 10 year old boy desperate to find his birth mother)

" **Hello Mrs. Wallace did you give birth to a son in 1945 in July?**"

"**No I have two daughters born in 1950 and 1954. What is this all about?**"

"Sorry Ma'am I was given the wrong information… "

Chapter 4.

On to Age 10.

After I left Wellington Street Public School I was sent to Connaught Intermediate School at the corner of Gladstone and Rosemount. There I did Grade 7 and 8.

Most of my classmates from the Wellington Street School ended up there as well, but there were a lot of the "upper crust" from the "Island Park Drive" area that looked down their noses at us "Lebreton Flats" punks. Of course, we assisted them in their derision as myself, I looked like John Travolta in the later movie "Grease" with my jet boots (complete with dangling chains) ducktail hairdo, sideburns below my ears and a real attitude.

This was inspired by Elvis Presley, now a rage with teenagers, having appeared on the Ed Sullivan show and grinding out the chart topping rock and roll songs. Us boys were acquainted to Brylcreem, a hair treatment you put in your hair after shampooing and your hair had dried. It smelled great and kept those ducktails and widow's peak perfectly in place.

You'd here the company jingle on the radio and TV almost everyday. It went something like this:

__Brylcreem a little dab'll do you,__
__But use it only if you dare,__

But watch out, the gals will all pursue yah!
They want to get their fingers in your hair....

In most of my classes there was this one girl that I became fascinated with. Brittany Hillis. She was the same age as me but she had developed early and I couldn't take my eyes off of her. She was the daughter of a high up official in the Bank of Canada and they lived in an "upper crust" home just off Island Park Drive. To make things worse she and her family attended Christ Church Cathedral so I saw her at school all week long and at Church on Sundays.

At this time in my life I was an Choir Boy at Christ Church Cathedral. You could be a Choir Boy with Duck Tails and Sideburns, just not the suitor of an upper crust girl near Island Park Drive.

There was another boy from the Island Park crowd that noticed I was paying special attention to Brittany. He decided in Metal Works class he would discourage me from my Brittany fantasy. We were making metal trays with square pieces of aluminum and after we rounded them we were going to etch a design in them with acid. I had my metal square in a vice preparing to round it off with shears. My tormentor decided to fix me, so he walked past me and when nobody was watching, grabbed my arm and rammed it to the 45 degree angle of metal protruding from the vice. It went all the way into the bone in my arm and the blood flowed like a river.

The teacher took me up to the school nurse who applied medication and bandaged me up. I was allowed to go back to class. On the way I went outside and did what any regular Lebreton Flats punk would do. I let the air out of the tires on his bike and bent his spokes out of shape. Took my Knife and ripped up his bicycle seat as well.

He stayed away from me after that. I still have the scar on my arm to this day.

Back then I started to be friendly with the Janitor of the church. His name was Jacques Thibadeau. He somehow recruited me for jobs at the church: such as washing the floors of the church and the big Meeting hall besides the Church. He had got cozy with my parents and they explained that Leslie was used to this kind of work so he enlisted me using their friendship as a hook.

He had found out from my parents that I was adopted and concocted a story that he actually knew my real Birth Mother. This was all lies but he played me like a violin. The next thing you know I was staying overnight sometimes at his apartment next door to the church. I was allowed to come and go as I pleased.

One night Jacques brought home his newest girlfriend. I was already asleep when they arrived. A few beers and whiskeys later they hit the sack. I was awakened in the middle of the night with grunts and groans and squeeking bedsprings. Then some French curses I had heard up by then like **"Tabernac!!" "Sacre Mere!!" "Colise!"** but these were words of sexual pleasure shouted out at the finalization of their coupling.

****

One night when I was there alone I phoned Brittany at home.

I had a major crush on her but she was destined to be my first major heartbreak. The night I called her up and professed my undying love for her and she informed me: **" You are a nice guy Leslie, but you'd never hit it off with my Dad. He would never approve of you with your leather jacket and jet boots and sideburns."** Then she said: **"Don't call here again"**.

At that time the Everly Brothers had a song on the hit parade that used to really hurt me big time everytime it played on the radio:

Don't want your love anymore,
Don't want your kisses that's for sure,
I die each time, I hear this sound....
Here he comes...... that's Kathy's clown
That's Kathy's clown...

Back at Connaught School I was not in a good mood. The student in front of me Bill Beattie, had this habit of leaning way back in his seat head extending into my space. I was in a particular foul mood one day after the Brittany rejection. I was looking at his head protruding into my airspace.

We had those desks with the slanted tops that had a hinge that stopped it at a certain point, but not before it could smash into a head protruding into my airspace. So all of a sudden, given my then frame of mind, I needed something in my desk that required my opening it to full extension of the hinge.

WHAM!! Head butt big time. Not too impressed. Beattie turned around and said: **"You're gonna regret that one Swartmann!"**

That next night as we rode home on the Street Car, I knew something was up. Beattie had recruited his buddy Jason to ride past Jason's stop and Beattie's stop until we got to my stop at Bronson Avenue. All three of us got off at the same time. I knew this was bad news and started to run the minute I got off the street car, but they caught up with me.

They both had 12 inch lengths of rubber hoses, knocked me to the ground and beat me all over with their rubber hoses. (It hurt like hell but didn't leave marks). When they finally let me go I ran home and told my Dad.

He called Beattie's father who was a Ottawa City Police Constable but wasn't very sympathetic.

****

Around this time my Mom and Dad decided they'd take me out to a dance at the Coliseum at Lansdowne Park on Bank Street. The CFRA Happy Wanderers were playing. When we got there the place was packed. After about an hour or so, Joe Brown announced that he wanted to get some volunteers to come up and sing in their "Amateur Segment". He asked for volunteers. My Dad stuck up his hand. "Poppa Joe" as he was called then said come on up, Mister. My Dad said: **"Not me: Sonny Boy here"**

"Is that his name? Sonny? Asked Mr.Brown.

"No, his name is Leslie and he's a good singer."

Joe Brown said: **"Come on up Leslie and sing us a song."** I was very shy and deferred but everyone encouraged me to get up on the stage.

After some coaxing I went up, very nervous with butterflies flying in different directions in my stomach.

Joe Brown said: **"What would you like to sing young lad?"**

I said:" **Do you know " Jambalaya" by Hank Williams?** "Of course, we do, let's do 'er."

Then he leaned over and said: **"I know you're nervous Leslie. Here's a little trick. Don't look at the audience. You see that red and white exit sign at the back of the hall, above the door. Sing to that exit sign."**

I said: **"OK Mr. Brown, I'll try that."**

The song went off without a hitch. I got a nice applause and couldn't wait to get off the stage.

But they insisted I do one more. I got up and asked Bob King if he new " Let it be me" by the Everly Brothers. **"Sure do!"** he said.

Away we went. About half way through the song I realized that Bob King was singing the back-up harmony (softly) on the choruses. It really sounded great.

When it was over, I left the stage. Mom and Dad were beaming their approval at me.

It's a night I'll never forget.

****

Back at the Cathedral my relationship with JacquesThibodeau took a turn for the worst when he gave me a lecture about what I could do with my life. I used to tell him that I was thinking about either becoming a veterinarian or an English teacher. He had a better idea for me whereby I could quit school and start making big money working for the Gangster element in Montreal.

I guess the church hadn't checked him out too carefully before they'd hired him as Sextant. He had been involved with some low-life criminal people in Montreal and Western Quebec. He had been very secretive about his past.

He told me:

"I can set you up in Montreal with the gangs… You can run errands, make big bucks, before you know it you'll be driving a fast car and have chicks doin' you every day!!"

I said to myself, boy, did I ever figure you wrong, man. No way am I interested in your bullshit plan for my future.

I parted company with Jacques Thibodeau that very day.

I was now abandoning my search or curiosity to find my biological mother. It occurred to me that my mother Jean Swartmann and I were very close and she was the only person in life I could really think of as my Mom. After all, she had loved and raised me from diapers to teenager. I would probably not like this other lady who had given birth to me. Meeting her would probably confuse and stress me out. And I didn't want to hurt my Mom's feelings either. I was very anchored in this family and couldn't imagine any other people besides Frank and Jean Swartmann as my parents.

I thought to hell with it, let sleeping dogs lie.

Chapter 5.

High School 1957

I wanted so bad to get in to Ottawa Technical High School because it was only a four minute walk from my home. But when I went to register they gave me a hard time. I had poor marks from Connaught School and several trips to the Principal's Office on my records.

So I was finally accepted but only if I accepted to go in with the lower grade students that were destined for Machine Shops, Auto Mechanics,etc.

This only lasted for 3 months. By then I was aceing all tests with 85% and 95% averages. So I was called down to the Principles office one day and informed that in my current classes/programme I wasn't "challenged enough". So I would be transferred to the "Pre-Engineering" programme.

Here I was thrown in with what were considered the "brains of the school". Interestingly enough there was a lot of challenge. But not in my favourite subjects.

Forget Math, Chemistry and Science. And French. Pass marks only. On French a fail.

But give me English Comp, English Lit, Geography and History and I aced it every time. When the other students were handing in the

"Hardy Boys" and "Huckleberry Finn" for Book reports I was turning in Shakespearean Plays. My English teacher Mr.Monk was soon very supportive and encouraged me. I was given an appreciation of the better classical authors and was soon reading Dickens, Somerset Maugham, Hemingway, Tolstoy and Dostoyevsky. My favourite book of all was "The Yearling" by Marjorie Kinnan Rawlings, not because she got the ~~Nobel~~ *PULITZER* prize but because I was always so tuned into Animals.

As a young boy I had read a book called "Uncle Tom's Paradise". It was all about a special heaven where dogs, cats and all animals went when they died.

High School at Ottawa Tech was an experience. I was a runt. 5 foot 8 inches 100 pounds you could count every one of my ribs. So the punks singled me out. They used to trip me in the halls between classes, throw my books around and laugh at me.

Right about then I hooked up with Angelo Santini. He was a big broad chested mustled Italian Stallion that had a hard time with my favourite subject "English Lit and English Comp". So we met at our spares in the cafeteria and I would coach him in his English Assignments. No Fees, but he had to buy me a Pepsi for the tutoring.

One day after I had had one of my bad experiences in the halls with the Lebreton Flats punks I was not in a good mood.

Angelo asked me: **What's the problem buddy?"**

I told him about the problem in the halls with the Lebreton Flats Punks.

I heard later that he located my tormentor (who was not much bigger than me) and Angelo picked him up by the throat, lifted him about 2 feet off the ground then opened an unused locker, jammed him into it, banged the locker door on him 3 or 4 times, then picked him out by the scuff of the neck and informed him in plain but broken Italian English:

Donta Fucka wita Swartmann No More!!!

Guess what? I never had a problem with the Lebreton Flats punks ever again.

It was then I got into music. The first thing I did was join the Ottawa Technical High School Band. The first instrument I wanted to learn to play was the saxophone. (It was used in almost all early rock and MoTown music.)

Unfortunately, I was told that you first learn the clarinet, then maybe we'll let you learn the sax. Reed instruments and I didn't hit it off. So I tried brass: first the trumpet. The trumpet and I didn't hit it off either. So I went for the Tuba. This was a joke, all I did with it was take it to Ottawa Tech football games and let out a huge **BLLAATTT!!** Whenever we scored a goal.

The OTHS Band and I soon parted company.

****

Years before we had formed a group of local boys in the neighborhood. Nowadays you'd call us a gang, but back then we were just 4 pre-teen boys that hung around together and met in our "clubhouse". This was an abandoned old storage shed at the base of Nanny Goat Hill. Nanny Goat Hill is located behind the St.Vincent de Paul Hospital on Cambridge Street. It runs all the way from the West side of Bronson avenue to Primrose close to Booth.

There was a ledge back then that you could walk along at the top of the cliff and if you slipped you would plunge more than 50 feet down to a rock bottom. Our initiation to the "club" was to walk this entire ledge to the end (without falling) and then we were "in". It was a heart-thumping experience but we   all did it unscathed.

As we grew older from pre-teens to early teens we started to notice attitude changes among our group. I was the poorest one of the bunch. My clothes and the fact that I never had any money made me a target for ridicule by Matthew Spence our so called leader. His father worked for the Federal Government and made a good income. Bill Beattie's father was a Constable in the Ottawa City Police Department and of course wasn't suffering financially. Bill never made fun of me so we grew closer as friends. Jason Spratt (the final member of the group and the other member of the earlier "rubber hose duo") was also well heeled as his father was an Accountant in the City of Ottawa Accounting office.

We started to dress the same. We all wore black jeans and black leather jackets. The others had new ones, but mine was an nearly new slightly worn out from the Neighbourhood Services after I bugged Mom and Dad into caving in and getting it for me for extra work I did around the apartment. We all sported sideburns and ducktail hairdos except Beattie as his cop father wouldn't allow it. But that was OK with us.

We also had a rule that we would each carry a knife. This was a cheap fish knife that had an imitation pearl handle and one very long blade that folded into the handle. The other guys bought them brand new. I got mine at a pawn shop for $1.00. We were never going to use them in a street fight but it made us feel superior and very dangerous dudes of the "Lebreton Flats" area.

As we advanced into our teen years, a day came when I knew the club was no longer for me.

I met all the guys at the clubhouse at the usual meeting time after supper. Matthew proposed his latest bright idea.

"Let's go roll a queer at Major Hill Park tonight!"

What the hell are you talking about ? I asked.

"It's simple. All four of us go down there and three of us hide in the bushes. One of us sits on a bench in the park like he wants to get picked up by a queer. He plays along with the queer when he hits on him and suggests they go into the bush and do the deed. When they get there we all jump on the queer, kick the shit out of him and grab his wallet and anything else worth taking... "

I said: **"Are you completely nuts? This is crazy! No way will I have anything to do with a bullshit plan like that. Don't you realize that that's a felony? You could end up in jail!"**

" Oh, Swartmann you're such a wuss! To hell with you, we'll do it without you. "

I looked at Bill Beattie (son of the Ottawa cop) and he looked very uncomfortable.

I said: "**I think there's more than just me not hot to trot for your bullshit plan**".

Bill said: "**Count me out, man…**"

I decided then and there that this club was no longer going to be part of my life so I told Matthew: "**I think I've had enough of you and this deal so I'm out of here, find somebody new to listen to your bullshit ideas.**"

Bill said: "**Count me out too, man.. "**

At this point Matthew flew into a complete rage (he had a bad temper that would be his downfall later in life).

His parting shot to me as I headed for the door was in his mind going to be the zinger of all zingers.

He said: "**Swartmann, you think you're pretty much a hot shot with the girls, right? Well you know what? You think you're a Casanova but really you're a Casanothing!**" Followed by a hearty haha.

Back then I had two modes. I would either be dumbfounded by a statement like that and totally unable to respond or I could come back with a really sarcastic response. On this particular occasion I was in sarcastic mode.

I said to Matthew: "**Yeah? Well let's check back in a couple of years and see who has the Casa and who ends up a nothing!**"

Then Bill and I headed for the door and I said: "**I'm outta here for good…** And Bill said "**Me too!**"

****

After that Bill and I became a "Club of two". We were inseparable. We even learned Morse Code so we could communicate at night after dark with flashlights. I would go up to my upstairs bathroom window and he would go to his kitchen window on his place on Wellington Street. Since I was up on the Nanny Goat Hill and he was downhill about a quarter mile, we could flash intermittently with our flashlights in Morse Code. (No text messaging or Internet back then). The messages were short and condensed such as: "**Get yr HW**

(homework) done? Answer : Yep. Gng (going) to bed now? Answer: Yep. OK , Night bud… " OK night… "

We decided at age 12 we were going to volunteer to be Sunday School Teachers at St. John's Anglican Church on Somerset Street. There was this girl, Angela, our age, short but very attractive and well developed for her age. She lived on Lyon Street and didn't attend our School. She went to Glashan which was a school down by Catherine Street. If you lived East of Bronson Avenue, you went to Glashan. If you lived West of Bronson you went to Connaught.

Bill was very stricken with her, but I made the first advance. I invited her out on a date. She liked to bowl so I said let's go bowling Saturday night. I picked her up at 6:30 and we walked down to Maple Leaf Bowling Lanes on Laurier Avenue past Bank Street.

The first thing I noticed as she paid very close attention to the amount of money I was spending on the date. When I paid for the bowling shoes rentals and bought us two pepsi's she was squinting hard at the cash register like she was mentally recording my cash expenditures for our date. Later when we finished bowling I paid for my time in the alleys and she was squinting again at the cash register. After that I took her to a restaurant at Bank Street and Laurier and we bought Milk Shakes. Again, as we left and I was paying the cashier, she was squinting at the cash register.

I thought this is my first and only date with you, girl. I walked her home, took her right up to her door then I shook her hand and said: **" It was real nice, goodnight, I'll see you around… "**

She had a somewhat shocked look on her face but I didn't stick around for any further conversation. As I left her place I thought, *never in a million years would I date this girl again.*

Bill wanted to know how our date went. I told him it was a disaster, worst date I was ever on in my life!

He said: **"Mind if I ask her out?"**

I said: **"Be my guest, man!"**

He dated her once, then twice, then a third time. Next thing you know they were going steady. Later in our late teens he asked me what I thought about it if he was to propose to Angela.

I said: **"Fill your hat, Man….. if she turns your crank, go for it."**

Sure enough, he finished high school, got hired onto the Ottawa Fire Department and the next thing you know, they were getting married. But guess what? I wasn't invited to the wedding. I guess Angela didn't feel I was good company for my erstwhile buddy Bill Beattie.

Earlier though, Bill had been saving his allowances and money he'd earned on weekends. We heard that a friend of the family had a Chevvy sedan for sale, cheap. It was a plain jane 6 cylinder with standard transmission with the gear shift on the steering column. Back then we called that "3 on the tree"

We went to this fellows place and looked the car over. It was in decent shape a little rust here and there, but seemed a good deal for $500. We asked if we could take it for a test drive. The fellow said he'd need a deposit and us to sign a "conditional sales contract". He disappeared into his house and came out a few minutes later with this handwritten contract.

We asked how much of a deposit? 10% …. Fifty bucks. Bill signed the form and handed him the money. We then started up the car and went on our test drive. This was really to get the car down to a garage where Bill's uncle worked as a mechanic.

We had noticed that there was a slight pinging noise in the engine. When we got to the garage, Bill's Uncle gave it the once over.

After a thorough inspection he turned to Bill and said: **"My advice to you Bill is don't buy this car…"**

"Why not?" We asked.

"Well for one thing, The frame is almost rusted through, but better yet that ping ping ping you hear is the death rattle of the engine. It's about to throw a piston. Take it back Bill and keep looking."

So we took the car back and told the owner no sale and we'd like our fifty bucks back.

"Sorry fellows, that was a non-refundable deposit." He said.

"What kind of bullshit is that?" I asked.

He said: **"Tell your friend there to read what he signs before he signs a contract. It clearly stated the deposit would not be refunded if you backed out of the deal."**

We headed straight home to Bill's place. He asked his Dad if that guy could get away with ripping us off like that?

His Dad said: **"Caveat Emptor.."**

We said: **"What does that mean?"** Bill's Dad said **"That's Latin for "BUYER BEWARE".** And then he said, I guess to rub it in even further: **"There's an old saying that goes "There's a sucker born every minute…"**

Bill took his $450 and put it back in his Bank account.

Chapter 6.

Now about Leslie the Farmer....

Since I was no longer interested in religion based summer camps and was developing an independent streak, after school ended in June I started looking in the Ottawa Citizen an the Ottawa Journal for a summer job.

There wasn't a lot out there for a 13 year old boy, but I did notice farmers out in Metcalfe and Vars were advertising for summer students to work on their farms in the haying and oats season.

I got an interview out in Vars with a farmer who raised Dairy cows, pigs, chickens and geese. My Dad drove me out to meet him and after he looked me over he said to my Dad " **He's kinda small for his age?**" My Dad replied: " **He can probably outwork guys twice his size!**"

So I was hired at $10 per week plus room and board.

I got up at 5:00 a.m. every morning and we did chores until about 8:00 a.m. This consisted of feeding the chickens, pigs, cows and horses (two teams), milking the cows either by hand or a "Surge" gas powered milking machine then separating the cream from the milk with a hand powered separator. We usually got two enormous pails of cream that it was my job to carry from the barn to the house (several hundred feet) then down into the basement and dump them into big several gallon metal Dairy containers. At first I could never make to the house without making several stops to rest my aching arms. Within a few weeks I could make it all the way non-stop. At the end of the trip, that's when I got my secret bonus.

Whenever I poured the Cream into those big metal Dairy containers, I always left about a cupful in the pail for sampling. It was pure cream still warm straight from the cow (not homogenized or pasteurized) but I glugged it down about 2 cups per day.

Did I ever put on the pounds that summer.

In the morning after chores we came into the farmhouse and had breakfast. Some mornings it was fried baloney & eggs. Then it could be pancakes with Corn Syrup. Lots of toast. They were poor farmers, no electricity, no phone, lights by coal oil lanterns. This wasn't unusual to me as my Grandma and Aunt in Denbigh lived in the exact same conditions as did my cousins the Neumans up in Hardwood Lake.

During the day, we fixed fences, built granaries, repaired the Barn, worked in the hay, cleaned the pig pens and chicken houses and weeded the gardens.

My boss Ernie used to cultivate the potatoes with a big Clydesdale mare. He'd hook her up to the harness and would go up and down the rows of potatoes, plowing all the weeds underground with his ancient tiller. One day he said to me: "**The horses seem to like you a lot, do you want to try tilling these potatoes with Jesee?**"

I said sure and gave it a try. The horse was so used to this job I didn't have to do anything but guide the tiller. She knew when to turn at the end of the row and away we went, no exertion on my part other than to guide the tiller. Ernie said: **"Looks like you just inherited my favourite job!"**

Ernie was a strange man. He was in his fifties, never had married and lived with his two older spinster sisters on the family farm. I could never figure out why he never married as he was handsome in his own way.

One night when I was in the village of Vars, I asked a local why didn't Ernie ever marry. I was informed that when he was young he caught the mumps and they "went down on him" so he could never father any children.

Ernie and his sisters rented a 100 acre vacant farm about 3 miles from their place. Here they planted hay every second year. Ernie and I would go up there early each day with both teams of horses. I would operate the mower and he would rake the hay into rows.

One week we went to Embrun to the sale barn to sell our piglets. I had my $10 bill in my pocket and saw a jersey calf that looked kind of scrawny. I could buy it from the farmer for, of course, ten bucks.

So I asked Ernie if I bought the calf could we bring it back to the farm and I'd take care of it and fatten it up. He thought it was a stupid idea but I bugged him enough he relented and said: **"If she gets sick I ain't paying for no vet!"**

We brought her home and nursed her back to health. She got friendly with a Guernsey cow that kind of adopted her. I told Ernie that I was glad that we nursed her back to health but when the time came for me to go back to school he could have her as I couldn't have a Jersey Calf in downtown Ottawa. Plus she would give him very rich creamy milk after she freshened.

When I worked the horses on the mower Ernie gave me strict instructions:

" Every few rows, give 'em a rest, that's the hardest piece of machinery that they pull! Give them some water, see how they sweat pulling that mower?"

"Yes Sir", I said.

One day, late in the afternoon, Ernie said **"Those horses worked hard enough today, hitch them up to the Buckboard and take them home, then water them and give them their supper, they deserve it."**

I was happy with that news and unhitched them from the mower and hitched them up to the Buckboard. Then I looked forward to a leisurely ride slowly at a walk pace back home.

But this was not to be. As I made it about halfway to the farm a bunch of teenagers came along in their hot rod car churning up dust and gravel and laid on the horn as they swung out to pass us. I was hitched to a mare and a gelding that didn't get along at the best of times. The teens spooked the horses and they broke into a gallop.

I pulled on the reins as tight as I could yelling **"WHOA.. WHOA BACK!!"**

As loud as I could but there was no stopping them. At one point I decided I'm not going to get out of this alive, my heart was pounding in my chest and I figured this is the big one Swartmann, you're done like dinner. Somehow I finally reined them in about a mile past the farm after a two mile joy ride.

I sat there for about ten minutes until I stopped shaking and my heartbeat returned to normal. Then I turned the buckboard around and returned to the farm.

That night I not only fed and watered them I gave them a rubdown with soapy water and rinsed them off because they had spared my life. Those horses and I became best of friends.

That week I took my weeks pay $10 and bought a guitar from a kid that wanted to trade his guitar for beer. Now I could get my fingers around the neck!!

So at the end of the day I could practice my guitar. I found a book about basic chords so the first song I learned to play was "Hello Walls" by Faron Young.

No big deal. D Chord A major C major and G minor. Loved it. Then I worked on a lot of Hank Williams Sr. songs which were mostly G C D major.

In the middle of the summer there was a new addition to the farm.

Ernie and his sisters had arranged a foster home placement from the Children's Aid Society. Here was their chance to have a full-time farm hand 12 months of the year.

Problem was he was a jerk. Not that Ernie and the sisters ever noticed. He was their salvation. We used to say back then "lazier than a pet racoon". This kid was worse than that. Even the animals didn't like him. The geese used to chase him and snap at his feet. The farm's dog snarled at him whenever he came near. The horses crowded him if he got in their stalls.

I ended up doing all the work and he got all the praise. I finally had enough of this job but had suffered so much abuse from him and the rest of them that I finally decided to exit stage right but first I needed some revenge.

My last night on the farm, I had packed up all my clothes and stuff to go back home to Ottawa and hid it under the porch.

After supper we had gone out to do the night chores and the last thing was to slop the pigs with skim milk and mash. Ernie had gone back to the house leaving Bozo (that was my nickname for the jerk) and I to finish slopping the pigs. It was dusk and I said to Bozo: **"You ever see what happens when you piss on an electric fence like this one around the pig stall?"**

He said: **"No, what?"**

I said: **"the sparks fly up just like the fourth of July!!!**

"Really?"

Yah man, it's spectacular!

"Wow! Here goes!"

So he unzipped his zipper pulled it out and proceeded to pee on the electric fence, which of course sent 10 or 15 volts of electricity into his private parts.

Did I feel bad? **NOT!!**

I did the hundred yard dash up to the porch, collected my things and started the long trek back to Ottawa.

That night there was no one on the road. I had to walk about 15 miles to highway 17 and Carlsbad Springs at which point I hitched a ride right into downtown Ottawa.

I finally made it home, climbed into my familiar bed and explained the next day that I wasn't cut out to be a farmer.

Chapter 6.

Back in Ottawa...

I went through Grade 9 and 10 at Ottawa Tech and then I decided school wasn't for me. I wanted to quit and go out to work. Back then you could quit High School early with your parent's permission. I brow beat them constantly until they gave in and signed the necessary papers.

My first job was with CN Telegraphs. They needed delivery boys with bikes. I had this old girl's bike that a tenant gave me for free years before so I hired on to be a telegraph delivery boy. I knew Ottawa backwards so I never wasted time finding my delivery homes. Mostly I remember delivering a lot of telegrams to Embassies in Sandy Hill and off of the Rideau Canal near Bronson Avenue.

This was OK right up until the snow flied. It was an early winter that melted away real fast but not fast enough to not sicken me with the idea of what a lousy job this would be going into the winter.

So I got out the Citizen and the Journal and checked the want ads. Lo and behold they were recruiting "special sales reps" for MacLean Hunter Publishing. No experience necessary! Great potential earnings! Be your own boss!

I fell hook line and sinker. Now I was going to make the big bucks! *Someday my day will come.*

I'll watch my ship as it sails in,
And my pockets won't be filled with sand,
And my cup will overflow....
From a song by George"No show" Jones aka "The Possum"

Too bad I was so gullible and impressionable at that age. Here was a "supervisor" would show me all the ropes, how I would make the big bucks hawking subscriptions to various magazines to a target audience. His name was Josh Williams and he was in his late 20's but had a baby face that would pass for late teens.

He started off working me through apartment buildings. We had this line to start out the sales conversation, that we were University Students trying to raise funds for our tuition, but our parents were poor and couldn't help us out financially. That's why we hoped they could look at our list of publications, such magazines as MacLean's, Chatelaine, Time, various sports magazines, religious magazines, we had them all. All they had to do was sign a 1 year subscription.

In Ottawa it went well. I was well received, I looked the part and signed many subscriptions. So I had built up a lot of false confidence in my abilities in this marketing project.

What I failed to see at my early age was why was this hot shot supervisor Josh living in a cheap apartment on Metcalfe Street, didn't own a car, not wearing a very fancy wardrobe, but he and I were going to rake in the dough, selling subscriptions for MacLean Hunter!

The next thing he was talking me into going to Newfoundland. That's were his wife and family were, he was just on a temporary assignment in Ottawa and I would make a fortune on "the Rock". When I told Mom and Dad they weren't too impressed but consented based on the fact that I'd been fairly successful selling these subscriptions in Ottawa making much more money than the Telegram job.

So with a hundred dollars we ventured down to Cambell's Ford used car lot on Laurier avenue just past Bank Street.

There was a clunker there for $75.00. No safety. As is where is, no Warranty. He bought it. We loaded our stuff in the car and away we went on our way to Newfoundland. We got all the way through Vanier just past St.Laurent Blvd. at the Maple Leaf Hotel when our vehicle gave up the ghost. **Splutter, splutter, BANG!**

Deader than a doornail. We grabbed our stuff worth carrying and abandoned the deceased vehicle.

At this point we/he decided we could hitchhike to Newfoundland. After all we could sell subscriptions on the way down and finance our trip. We lucked out on our first ride. All the way to Montreal.

That's where everything went downhill.

It seemed like we walked through half the Metropolitan Freeway until a Trucker picked us up as he pulled up an on-ramp. He took us as far as Cap de Madeleine, Quebec, the end of his ride. This was on the other side of Trois Rivieres on the North Shore of the St.Lawrence River.

Josh decided we needed to go and relax in the local pool hall. I was hungry but Josh told me to be patient. We sat down and watched a few patrons as they played snooker. What I didn't realize was that my boss Josh was a world class pool shark and was studying the players to determine who was a potential source of money. A mark.

He eventually had sized up the players and struck up a conversation with one of them. One of the group spoke broken English and it was decided who would play who for money. He played the first player and won hands down. He was building up his war chest, but sucking the other fellows in in the process. He chose the easiest person to beat first. Took his money, prepared to lose most of it with the middle player. This would spurn the best player to challenge him and bet the big bucks to beat him. I knew French much better than Josh but acted like I was strictly English speaking.

In the background conversation I heard such comments as " **These are them mon dieu anglais from Ontario**" and " **we'll show them anglais how to play pool!**"

So the set up was complete. He suckered their best player to two games, raising the stakes after he beat him the first time so their hero could redeem himself then trashed him on the last game for major bucks (back then I think he won $50 starting off with $5.)

At this point we exited stage right on the excuse that we had an appointment to keep in St.Foy.

On the way out of town there was a chip wagon and we hunkered down with Burgers and Fries and of course, Pepsi Cola.

Then came Quebec City. Our ride took us past the bridge to the south shore. We ended up in downtown Quebec City. We asked around and discovered that there was a ferry across the river to Levis. We made our way to the dock and soon discovered there was a toll to ride on the ferry even as a walk-on passenger.

This is when I discovered that my travel mate was not only a pool shark, but also a con-man. We went down to the docks and inquired as to the cost of the ferry ride. There was a sympathetic looking Truck driver with an Ontario plated Delivery truck waiting in line to put his truck on the ferry.

Josh said to me in a loud voice; **"Hey man we can't afford this ferry! We're going to have to go back and walk over the bridge back there!"**

The truck driver heard Josh and asked: **"Where are you guys headed?"**

Josh answered: **"St.John's Newfoundland"**

The trucker said "You're a long way from home.."

He then said if you guys don't have the fare to cross on the ferry why don't you get in the back of my truck with the cargo. They won't count you if you're not sitting up in the cab and they never check my cargo hold.

So we jumped into the back of the truck, he closed up the roller door and when he opened it up we were on Highway 20 on the south shore of the St.Lawrence River. The driver said you can stay with me to Cabano, that's where I drop my load.

Next stop Cabano, just outside the New Brunswick border. Here it was a major snow storm so we parked ourselves in an all night Truck stop and watched for a Trucker that could take us on our next leg.

We didn't get a trucker but we did get (my) worst nightmare.

A 1956 Ford Crown Victoria rolled into the truck stop. The driver got out and came in to buy some smokes and two large bottles of Ginger Ale.

He looked around the stop and spotted us. We were obviously not Truckers and he asked: **"Do either of you dudes own a driver's license?"**

Josh said: **"I got a Newfoundland Driver's License"**

"That's good in all Canada so would you like to drive me to Fredericton I've been driving for hours and I need a replacement Driver for a while... "

"Sure, be glad to, but my buddy comes along for the ride?"

"No problem, Let's go!"

This is where things go from bad to worse. We piled into the Crown Vicky, I went into the back seat, curled up and fell fast asleep. As I slept the miles melted by. They drove through Edmundston, Grand Falls, Hartland, Woodstock and eventually arrived in Fredericton.

I had been asleep the whole time and didn't realize that the Crown Vicky guy and Josh were nursing a 40 ouncer of Seagram's VO from Cabano to Fredericton.

By the time we got to Fredericton and our ride dropped us off in downtown Fredericton, it was about 9:00 p.m.

I was just waking up to the fact that our ride was over and we had made it all the way to Fredericton when I realized something was seriously wrong with my travel mate. He seemed delirious which I attributed to a lack of sleep. As we walked down the street, he all of a sudden decided to walk up the laneway to this house and bang on the door.

I said: **"What the hell are you doing?"**

He said: **"We're home! I want Doris to let us in?"**

I explained to him that he was confused, we weren't in St.John's we were in Fredericton, New Brunswick. A lady came to the door and told him to get the hell off her property or she'd call the cops. I grabbed his arm and led him away.

The next thing I knew he had this sudden burst of energy and headed up a side street where looking ahead I could see a Irving Oil Fuel Oil truck filling up the oil tank of this large mansion-type residence.

Josh was weaving around as he walked and I was having a hard time to catch up to him and then the worst of all developments occurred. He hung a hard left at the laneway of that mansion, went right up to the front door (which was unlocked) and walked right in.

I was beside myself. What to hell? What am I supposed to do in a situation like this?

I was brought up to always tell the truth and face the music, my Dad and Mom had taught me it's the best way to go.

So based on my limited knowledge of the situation I went up to the front door of that house and rang the bell.

An Elderly gentleman, very distinguished looking opened the door and said:

" Yes, Young man, what can I do for you?"

I said something like: **" Excuse me Sir, But my friend just walked into your house and I don't know where he is but he's probably delirious because we've been on the road hitchhiking since Ottawa and he's probably right out of it."**

The elderly gentleman was dressed in pajamas and a velvet housecoat and invited me in. We started to search the house and eventually found Josh in this person's guest room curled up on the bed in a fetal position.

The homeowner called the Fredericton Police Department and it seemed in second's a Black & White arrived lights flashing, no siren.

The police came in picked up Josh and put him in the back of the cruiser and asked me what I was going to do. I said that I was on my way to Newfoundland with him and would it be OK if I stuck with him as they took him down to the Police Station. That was agreed so I rode in the back seat with Josh on the way to the station.

As we drove along in the cop car the police asked me a few questions, the first one being did I not realize that my buddy was drunk? I said no, I thought he was delirious. Then I explained that I slept all the way from

Cabano to Fredericton. **"Yah, but didn't you pick up on the stink of him?**

"No sir, I didn't."

"Do you realize whose house he walked into?"

"No sir I don't know, who is it?

"That's Judge Mark Matheson's house, the Chief Magistrate of Fredericton, your buddy made a seriously bad choice of houses to invade!!!"

Anyway they explained they were booking Josh for a number of counts: Drunk and Disorderly Conduct, Illegal entry, and Vagrancy and he would have to appear in court tomorrow in front of guess who: Judge Matheson".

When we got to the station the two officers asked me what I was going to do now, where was I going to stay. I said I would like to stay with him , I know he screwed up but I got to stick by him. They explained that he's going into the "drunk tank".... You don't want to go there... I said It's OK, just let me stick with him, I want to be sure he's OK, we still have a long way to go.

That night I was introduced to "the drunk tank". There were 4 people in 4 cells. Josh in one, me next door and two others. Of the other two, one had pissed his pants so we had stifling heat plus urine smell. The other occupant had puked up all over himself but it wasn't contributing to the aroma as the urine guy.

In this particular drunk tank the bed was a steel slab with holes in it. I guess there was no point putting on a mattress as the visitors would have either pissed, puked or shit on them.

So I took off my coat, my shirt, my Tshirt and made a pillow. I was so tired I fell asleep in minutes.

About midnight I woke up and I noticed one of the cops was standing outside my cell. He asked me: **"When was the last time you ate, young lad?"**

I told him I had a Hamburger in Cabano yesterday. He disappeared for a few minutes and brought me back half of his egg salad sandwich from his lunch box and a can of Seven-Up from the Coke machine.

It was at that point I finally started to appreciate Policeman and viewed them in a different light than I had up until then.

The next morning I woke up at 5:30 a.m. I ached all over my ribs from sleeping on that steel slab all night. Josh was totally dead to the world and so I rattled my door to see if I could get out for some fresh air. Had to get away from the urine, puke stink out into the real world.

The Officer on duty said sure, we're not holding you, just your friend : You're free to go…

So out I went into the cool crisp November morning. There was a fog not yet burned off by the sun. Everybody it seemed in Fredericton was still asleep accept business owners.

As I walked down the main Street I noticed there was a Restaurant with it's light's on already. It advertised " Chinese and Canadian Foods".

I walked in and there was only one person in the restaurant. It was the owner, an older Chinese businessman sitting at a back table with bunch of books, doing calculations. He looked up at me and said: **"What you want, boy?"**

I told him my sad story how I was stuck here in Fredericton, no money my chum was in jail, hadn't eat much in a couple of days. Did he have any jobs I could do for food?

The old Chinese guy smiled and said : **"Where you from, boy?"**

I said **"Ottawa"**.

"You long way from home. You know how to wash floors?"

"Show me the mop and pail and I'll show you how I can wash floors,"

I was introduced to the pail with rolling wheels the mop and told if I washed the kitchen floor and the customer aisles in the restaurant I could order anything I saw on the menu.

When I was finished he was so pleased he said **"What you want off menu Ottawa boy?"**

I told him I'm really partial to hot chicken sandwiches. He said: **"I fix you myself right now!"**

Never in my life had I ever seen a hot Chicken Sandwich like this. This would be fit for a Trucker or a Lumberjack. There was two pieces of white bread in between there was at least an inch of pure white meat chicken, smothered in gravy, besides a bunch of French fries I could never have eaten, plus cole slaw. Add to that a glass of milk in a Milk shake container.

When I was finished I thanked him up and down and he said: " **You ever come this way again, stop in, you good worker, Leslie!**

As I as leaving I asked him if he could lend me a couple of smokes? The owner "Mr.Lee" said: " **What you smoke Leslie?**" Back then it was Export "A" . He grabbed a pack off the counter and said.: " **A small bonus Leslie, maybe you come back someday, I hire you…** "

The next day was Josh's trial in court. I asked the cops what kind of fine are we looking at, here?

They said: That depends on his frame of mind. He's a fair Judge but your buddy invaded his home. On the other hand he was impressed with you your honesty and your loyalty to your partner although misplaced since you didn't clue in to the fact that he was drunk.

The Trial proceeded. The Court Clerk read into the record: "Josh Williams, you are accused of Disorderly Conduct, Illegal Entry and Vagrancy, How do you plead?"

Josh said: "Guilty on all counts, your honour"

Judge Matheson then said: "**Why shouldn't I throw the book at you young man?**"

Josh said: "Your honour, I'm just trying to get back home to my wife and kids in Newfoundland. We hitched a ride in Cabano and the guy in the car asked me to drive to Fredericton, meanwhile we shared a bottle of whiskey on the way down. My buddy Leslie was asleep in the back seat as we had been hitch-hiking from Ottawa for three days. He didn't realize I was drunk and disoriented when we got into Fredericton. I'm sorry for what I did and promise I will not let this situation ever happen again. All Leslie and I want to do is to get to Newfoundland."

Judge Matheson looked at me and then said as follows:

" I probably should have excused myself from this case as it is a very obvious conflict of interest. On the other hand, I have to admit I am impressed with this young fellow Leslie. He did the right thing. He stepped up to the plate and spoke the truth. This is something we want and hope for in all our children. As to you, Josh Williams, I'm not too impressed with you as a person. I hope you appreciate this young man you are travelling with. Anyway, I got up on the good side of the bed today and I am dismissing all charges with no fines. You will have to pay the Court Clerk $20 for court costs. Case Dismissed!"

I couldn't believe my ears. But then this was 1960 and Judges used their brains not like in the years ahead.

My next stop was the CN Telegraph office. I wired Josh's boss in Toronto and explained he needed a cash advance on Commissions he would earn in NFLD. Please wire us $50.

Lo and behold in came a wire transfer of $50 so I paid the $20 court fee and bailed out Jason.

****

Back on the road. We started out from Fredericton our next goal was Sydney NS in Cape Breton Island. That's where you catch the ferry from North Sydney to Port aux Basques Newfoundland on the "William Carson" the biggest ship I'd ever seen in my life.

Before we got there we were dropped off on the middle of a hill in New Glascow, Nova Scotia. We were let off on a major downhill slope, the whole town was built on a big hill!) So we looked across the street and there was the restaurant we needed. It advertised **"Biggest Burgers in NS!!!"**

My travel mate was back in con-man mode and said lets go get some free Biggest Burgers in NS!

He said you go in and put on your best down in the dumps face. They fall for it every time. **"Here's what you will say"**

I walked up to the owner and said my buddy and I were famished we were hitch hiking to Newfoundland and did they need any dishwashers as we didn't have money but we would be willing to work for a Hamburger and some fries. I guess she took pity on us as she took us into the kitchen and pointed us to trays full of dirty dishes, cups and knives, spoons and forks. Clean this up and you eat, she said.

About an hour later we emerged from the kitchen. The owner checked out our work, seemed satisfied and yelled back an order to the Cook. Minutes later there was two supersized Hamburgers with the works and two plates of French Fries drowning in Beef gravy. And two chocolate milk shakes. It was like I died and went to Heaven.

From here on it got much worse.

We managed to pick up a ride from New Glascow in a big rig 18 wheeler headed to Sidney, NS. He was a great guy, typical of truckers back then and talked us all the way short of Sydney. Then he said :"Sorry guys but I'm going to have to pull over and take a restbreak, been truckin' now for 24 hours. As we sat there letting him have his much needed sleep we listened to his truck radio that was able to pick up Charlottetown PEI radio. They were playing Don Messer and the Islanders with Marg Osborne and Charlie Chamberlain.

Finally our Trucker woke up. He **said " Sorry you guys, I needed that otherwise" I might have lost it falling asleep at the wheel!"....**

Our next leg took us into Sydney. But we wanted to get to North Sydney where Josh had family and friends.

We got off the eighteen wheeler at a 24 Truck stop/restaurant.

It was now 5:30 in the morning. After we downed a coffee and an order of toast, a Sydney Times delivery truck rolled in to get their coffee fix from Sydney to North Sydney. Of course , Josh clued into the situation immediately and in no time flat we were riding in the back of a delivery truck full of Newspapers destined to North Sydney

When they dropped us off in North Sydney he found his way to his cousin's home in the least side of town. I guess I should have clued in right then and there but I was still on the roll that I was going to make the "big bucks" on the Big Rock".

The next day we made our way to the ferry dock. We boarded the "William Carson" the biggest ship I'd ever seen in my life. Apparently I was told they drove to trains into the belly of the ship. Then they loaded the transport trucks on level 3 Passenger cars on level 2. Passengers on Level 1.

The trip started up fine until about half way into the 100 mile voyage. Right after we left the dock I found a bench to lay down on and fell asleep immediately. When I woke up were half way to Port Aux Basques in the middle of the Cabot Straight (It is approximately 100 miles from North Sydney to Port Aux Basques.) The sea wasn't quiet that night and it rolled and pitched the boat. My stomach started churning and the next thing you know I was running as fast as I could to the public washroom. I then talked to "Ralph on the Great White Telephone" for what seemed forever.

I was so glad when I finally saw shoreline. It meant I could get off that ferry and stand on solid ground that didn't move under your feet. We started hitchhiking again.

****

Our first lift took us to Cornerbrook. After walking about 2 miles we were picked up by a Station Wagon with a young couple with two toddlers. There was room for us as this was a Ford Country Squire a huge vehicle with plenty of seating space. We pulled into a gas station that displayed a sign that read: "LAST GAS STOP FOR 100 MILES".

There was absolutely nothing between Cornerbrook and Deer Lake, just road with bush and plains on both sides. About half into this jaunt we encountered three Moose in the middle of the road. There was a huge bull and two cows. I guess they figured they owned the road as they weren't getting out of the way. The man driving decided to lay on the horn. This didn't go over big with the big bullmoose and he snorted and pawed the ground with his foot. Josh advised the driver that he better get ready to floor it as the Bull was **"Getting pissed off at you!"**

One of the cows seemed upset by the aggressiveness of the bull and started to walk off into the ditch. It created an opening just wide enough to get the car through. Josh yelled: **"THREAD THE NEEDLE AND FLOOR IT!!"**

With gravel and dust spewing up and the sound of that big V8 revving up we went through that gap before the Bull had time to react. We were past the trio and gaining speed and looked back. The Bull was charging us with his antlers down and obviously in a very bad mood. But he couldn't keep up with Henry Ford's invention and we sped off to Deer Lake, Newfoundland.

From Deer Lake we picked up another ride to Badger. We spent most of half a day thumbing for rides but no takers. Then we noticed a train pulling into the station. We checked and it was headed to Grand Falls. Josh said **"Let's hobo our way to Grand Falls"**

I wasn't sure what that meant but soon found out. We went around the back of the train and found an empty boxcar. We jumped in and huddled in a corner out of sight. The train started to move and we figured we had aced it until we got just outside of Grand Falls. The train slowed down as it entered the Grand Falls Train yards and before we were able to jump out of the boxcar a guard spotted us.

He was very nasty at first, but Josh turned on the Newfie charm. He explained that we had hitchhiked all the way from Ottawa to get back to his home in St.John's. The guard softened and said: I need to collect standard fare from Badger to Grand Falls to Badger which was $10 each. We explained we were broke. He asked if we had anything of value?

In my packsack I had a German Made Solingen hunting knife in a leather sheaf that I had bought in a pawn shop in Ottawa. Brand new it would be worth about $100 back then but I had bought it for $25 after a lot of dickering with the pawnshop owner. It was one of my prized possessions but I figured if it kept us out of trouble (jail?) maybe I should part with it. It was well worth the $20 fare and I noticed the guards eyes lit up when I pulled it out of the scabbard.

He said: **I'm OK with the knife, but don't you guys pull this stunt again or I'll throw the book at yah"**....

We got off the train and headed to the outskirts of town. No rides for four hours but then a Cab Driver in a cab marked "Gander Taxi" screeched to a stop just past us and reversed himself back. He got in a conversation with Josh and it so happened he'd been driving straight for

24 hours, had just dropped off a fare from Gander to Grand Falls but was dead tired. He asked Josh if he had a Driver's License. Josh replied: **"I've got a Newfoundland Driver's License!"**

The deal was set. Josh took the wheel, The cab driver took the passenger seat and I curled up in the back seat, falling asleep almost instantly. That's the last thing I remembered until I heard this major banging noise followed by a crash and a major hissing noise. I sat up and saw we were not driving anymore, we were off the road suspended on a pile of firewood that had been stacked beside the road against a tree and the hood of the Pontiac cab was crushed into the tree. The radiator had exploded and there was steam pouring out of the front of the car.

The cabbie woke up and said: **"What da Christ?"**

Josh explained that he'd swerved to miss a moose (but I figured he just fell asleep at the wheel).

The two way radio still worked so the Cabby called his dispatcher and explained he swerved to miss a moose and wrecked the cab. I remember the Dispatcher sounded quite aggrevated with this news. He agreed to send a tow truck and we could hear him muttering under his breath as he reached and switched off his microphone: **" Lard tunderin' Jayzus!"**

We rode back in the towed wreckage into Gander. The Cab stand was very close to the Gander International Airport.

We bid goodbye to our Cabby and walked over to the Airport Terminal. By now it was 3:00 o'clock in the morning and the Terminal was totally empty. I found a bench and curled up and fell asleep almost instantly again.

During the night, Josh had been chatting up the Airport employees and discovered that there was a security guard who was driving to St.John's after his shift. Josh talked him into a ride and at 6:00 a.m. we were on our way to St.John's.

On the way I noticed there were really interesting names of small towns between Gander and St.John's. There was "Come by Chance" and "Heart's Desire" and " Heart's Delight".

****

In a few hours we were in Downtown St.John's. Our ride dropped us off right at Josh's house and I all of a sudden knew that all wasn't right in Paradise. As soon as Josh and I walked into the house, his wife Doris flew into a rage and they started argueing in very loud and colourful language. Mrs. Josh looked at me like I was a piece of garbage and I had this sudden feeling that I had been very stupid to sign onto this project.

The shouting continued so I decided to let myself out and I grabbed a cigarette from a pack on the table and said: **"I'm going outside for a smoke"**.

After a while the shouting seemed to calm down and eventually Josh came out and said that everything was cool now, you can come in Leslie. He said I could stay the night but he'd find me my own place the next day. Then we'd start making money!!

This was never to happen. Josh could sell the subscriptions left, right and center because he had the Newfie accent. On the other hand I talked like a "mainlander" and this turned off potential clients. The only people I could sell were drunks and mentally challenged persons that didn't realize what they were signing. This didn't sit well with me. If the only way I could make a living was conning people like that, I was not interested.

I decided enough was enough so I quit McLean Hunter and decided I better get back to Ottawa where I had a life. But this took some time. Now I was a vagrant 15 year old. I went to the UIC (Unemployment Insurance Commission) and looked at the jobs I could apply for. In most cases you needed to be 18. One job that caught my eye was an Assistant Chef trainee in Goose Bay Labrador.

I told the clerk at the UIC office that I'd lost my Social Insurance Card on the way down from Ottawa. She asked me my date of Birth so I told her July 2nd, 1941. She looked me up and down and decided I was 18 years old. (I hadn't shaved in a few days and I looked the part.)

Back then SIN cards were handwritten by the UIC clerks. So I walked out of there with an 18 year old Social Insurance Number Card. Goose Bay here I come! But it wasn't in the cards to land that job. I applied but was never accepted. My Ontario accent didn't help matters.

****

I was walking down Water Street the next day and noticed that a guy was following me. He looked like a foreign sailor and had a very angry look about him and he made me nervous.

As I rounded a corner I ran into a St.John's Policeman on his beat. I explained that I had been followed by a fellow that had me freaked out.

He started to question me after he heard my mainland accent and I blurted out the whole story about McLean Hunter, Ottawa to Newfoundland, arrival at Josh's home, the whole bit.

My opinion of Policemen was raised even another notch. This constable called into the station from a pay phone. Next thing you know a squad car rolled up. Don't worry Sonny you're not in any trouble, he said. They took me to the Police Station and I told them my story once again. When they realized I was only 15 years old with no means of support or money they explained that if I ended up stranded in Newfoundland they had a law or provision on the books that the Government of Newfoundland would pay my way back to my home province.

(Of course this was less expensive than putting me on their Welfare rolls).

I then met with some Judge who again read the report and signed an order to send me back to Ontario. The soonest means of Transportation was by plane, so I was booked on a flight the following week. Meanwhile I would be put up in a rooming house until the day of my flight.

****

Back then you could buy loose cigarettes at certain corner stores for one cent each. So my new hobby to fill my time before I was sent back to Ottawa was walking down the main streets in St.John's checking all the sidewalks for lost coins. I found enough to keep me in cigarettes most days.

Another taste of Newfoundland. They called cod "the fish" and back then there was plenty of them off the Grand Banks and it was the main diet of Newfoundland. We had Fish soup, broiled fish and fish burgers every day it seemed.

I had two experiences with the opposite sex in St.John's. One was very interesting, the other disgusting.

First, Interesting. There was this very attractive young lady that was checking out the want ads at the UIC office. She had red hair, sapphire blue eyes and skin like milk. I struck up a conversation with her and she liked my "mainland" accent. Before you know it we were going for walks and it looked like a relationship was to me in full bloom. One day we went to "Signal Hill" on the other side of the harbour. There were plaques on this old building that announced that this was the place where the first telegraph message was sent to England.

We were all alone in the building, no one else in site, so I made my move. I'd already kissed her the day before after I dropped her off home, but this time I not only kissed her, but grabbed her by her nice round bum.

She said: **"Paws off the merchandise, buddy!"**

I said: **"What's the problem here? Don't you like me?"**

"I like you lots but you're one of these here today, gone tomorrow guys and I know you're headed back to Ontario real soon. I don't want you leaving any reminders of your visit here in St.John's…"

"Reminders? What kind of reminders?"

"The kind that need their diapers changed and cry in the middle of the night!!"

I couldn't argue with that logic so I settled for a few more kisses and hugs and no more grabs where I wasn't invited.

Meanwhile back at the rooming house, the owner had a daughter that was in her early twenties grossly overweight and was a bar hopper and close friends with Screech, the national beverage of Newfoundland. I was bedded down on a fold down hide-a-bed each night and had been sound asleep for hours one night when the landlord's daughter came in half in the bag and horny for a shot at Leslie, the new guy.

I woke up to her crawling in bed beside me and putting her arm around me. She had undressed and was naked in bed with me. She stank of stale beer and body odour. I couldn't believe it. I muttered something like: **"I've got to go to the bathroom.."** and climbed out of bed.

I went to the bathroom and stayed there for about 15 minutes. Then I went back and listened at the door. Soon I heard snoring. There wasn't any place else in the house I could sleep so I crashed on the couch with a pillow I snuck off the hide-a-bed and curled up with an Afghan. I believe I slept that night with "one eye open" as I was sure I didn't need the Screech Queen taking another run at me.

One day I was sitting in the living room in the boarding house and the Jehovah Witnesses arrived at the door. The owner of the Boarding house didn't mind taking the Government's money but wasn't too crazy about her latest charge. So she decided she would sick the Jehovah Witnesses on me just to torture me.

Little did she realize I was bored stiff and this was just what I needed to flex my brain muscles. By age 15 I had read the Bible from cover to cover at least twice and could quote scriptures from the New Testament and Old Testament without even opening the Book.

They started in at me trying to convert me. They handed me their flyer and and asked me if I was a Christian.

I said **"Yes and probably a better one than you…"**

Why was that they asked. So I let them tell me their version of the Bible and every time they quoted something that suited their philosophy I would counter with another scripture that destroyed their point. They would read out of their Bible and I would quote them without the aid of the Bible. They finally realized there was "NO SALE" here and left.

I think my landlord had a better opinion of me after that. She had been eavesdropping outside the door during the meeting.

****

The next week I was due to leave the "Rock". I was booked on a TCA Viscount from St.John's to Ottawa via a stop over in Halifax. Back then it wasn't "Air Canada" it was " Trans Canada Airlines" hence TCA.

We flew out of St.John's and landed in Halifax, Nova Scotia. Our next leg took us to Montreal where they just managed to taxi in to Dorval Airport in advance of a major winter storm. There were no commuter flights to Ottawa so we were advised that we could either take the bus or wait out the storm, but we would require overnight accommodations which the airline wouldn't pay. Since I was broke I took the bus option.

Worst bus ride I ever was on for the rest of my life. After Hawkesbury, the bus had to pull over several times due to zero visibility. We finally arrived in Ottawa at 3:00 o'clock in the morning and I took the stop at the Chateau Laurier Hotel. This was about 8 blocks from my place.

Chapter 7.

Back home..

When I got off that bus I almost fell down and kissed the ground. There was Union Station. There was the War Memorial. There was the East Block. The Rideau Canal. It was snowing lightly now so I started on my 8 block walk.

I started to walk down Sparks Street and I noticed the Honey Dew Restaurant was still open. It was cold and blustery so I stepped inside. I had 20 cents in my pocket, not enough to buy anything. I was looking at the menu when this elderly man asked me what was my name. I told him and he said you look like you've had a rough ride.

Just got back home from Newfoundland, I said. Then I told him the whole story about Josh and McLean Hunter and he seemed really nice and offered to buy me a Honey Dew and a BLT.

This was a renowned hangout for the Ottawa Gay crowd but I (still gullible as ever) hadn't clued in. After I ate my BLT and drank my drink I thanked him and said I had to get back home now. He asked where I lived and so I told him and he said: **" I live two blocks from there. I'll walk you home!"**

He had an Apartment about two blocks from my home. As we got to his place on Cambridge Street he invited me in for a Pepsi. It wasn't long before I figured out that he was not just a nice guy trying to help me out, but a gay trying to hit on me. I made an excuse that I had to go to the bathroom. I waited in there with the door opened a crack and then he left the living room and made his way to the kitchen. When he opened the Fridge door to get something that's when I bolted and escaped through the door into the hall and out of his apartment building.

I ran full speed for at least one block then I slowed down to a walk. I drank in the smells of night in Ottawa as I approached my place. The key was in it's secret hiding place and I put it into the lock and sighed: **"Home at last".**

Mom and Dad were sound asleep so I didn't wake them. I went upstairs to my bedroom and there was my bed all neatly made with a note on the pillow that was in my Mom's handwriting and said: **We missed you Leslie We love you Welcome home XXX OOO**

****

The next day I got up and I noticed my Mom was glad to see me but Pop was another story. He started to rag on me first thing about what was my problem, didn't I realize this Josh guy was a con man, What are you going to do now? We can't afford to support you forever, get out there and get a decent job and pay your way around here, Sonny!!

So, that summer I got in a big fight with my Dad. I decided I couldn't live at home anymore so I was going to take off and visit or live with my cousins in Thessalon, Ontario.

My Mom was not impressed and was totally against the idea. Both my Grandma and Aunt Beatrice had passed on and my Mom was left the house in Denbigh since she was the oldest in the family.

My Mom said that I should not go to Thessalon. My Dad would mellow in time, why don't I go up and stay in Granny's place for the summer. He'll cool down by then and you can come back and do Grade 11 at Tech. You know how to cook and I'll send you $10 bucks a week for groceries.

Sounded like a plan to me. Mom had advertised my room to rent as a room and board deal. She had an instant response to her ad with a young Mountie named Robert Wilson. She collected Room & Board money and out of it got the $10 per week grocery money.

So she gave me the keys to Grandma's house and I packed a small bag of clothes and started hitchhiking to Denbigh. I did well all the way to Griffith, Ontario. Up until then I had got back to back rides from Ottawa to Renfrew, Renfrew to Dacre, Dacre to Griffith. Then I started walking. It's 10 miles from Griffith to Denbigh (nine miles to Grandma's house just outside Denbigh).

By the time I got there I was beat. My feet felt like they were ready to fall off my ankles. I was thirsty and hungry. I went into the old house and collapsed on the couch after I opened all the windows to air the place out.

I fell asleep and woke up in the pitch dark. There was no electricity or running water. I remembered there was always a coal oil lamp on the hutch beside the wood stove and where Grandma and Aunt Beatrice kept the wooden matches.

I stumbled around in the dark and found both. After I lit the lantern and sat back down on the couch. Then I noticed the radio. There was an old radio that was hooked up to a battery. When I switched it on a light came on and I found out it was tuned to Wheeling West Virginia, The WWV Jamboree. That was the favourite station in those parts. Sometimes late at night you could also pick up the " Grand Ole Opry" out of Nashville Tennessee.

The first few nights I had a hard time getting to sleep. I wasn't hearing the familiar sounds of Ottawa: Ambulance Siren's, Police car and Fire Truck sirens, Big Airplanes flying overhead to Uplands Airport, Transport Trucks and OTC buses rolling down Albert Street.

Instead I heard bullfrogs croaking, whippoorwills singing their plaintiff song and even wolves howling to each other back in the forest. Even the sound of the the creek steadily flowing and gurgling below the house.

After a few nights I adjusted and decided I preferred these sounds anytime over the big City Ottawa sounds.

The next day I decided I'd go visit my Aunt and cousins in Hardwood Lake. I could only do this by hitch hiking but since everyone knew my Aunt and Uncle I was there in no time.

They lived at the end of the road at Bruceton. It was a rundown farm in the middle of nowhere. But I loved My Aunt and Uncle and my cousins. They were the first that really accepted me wholeheartedly into the family. When I finally arrived, they were glad to see me. My Aunt had a nervous problem that her eyes wiggled back and forth at times when she was excited. We had supper and the two younger girls and I were on a couch. The oldest cousin was being much more friendly to me than my Aunt thought appropriate and everyone was called to bed upstairs.

During the night the wolves started howling. Not something a city kid from Ottawa was used to. I noticed Uncle Jethro had a gun over the mantle. It was a Winchester Carbine lever action.

I took it down and read on the stock that it was a 44-40 calibre. Enough to stop a wolf. Or for that matter, a Moose or a Bear!

It was fully loaded. I went back to my couch and went to sleep hugging my fully loaded 44-40. The sound of the wolves didn't bother me at all after that.

The next morning my Uncle was taking his team of Horses into the bush to skid out some logs for the sawmill at Chute.

My Aunt packed their lunch. It was homemade bread, with Bacon fat and brown sugar.

At noon I decided to pass on lunch and asked how could I get back to the main road and hitch back home. I was introduced to a cowpath or deer trail and informed... keep to your right all the time and you'll hit the road in about half a mile!

Lo and behold about 45 minutes later the main road appeared in all it's resplendent blacktop glory. I lay down in the ditch and waited for the sound of an approaching car or truck so I could hitchhike back to Grandma's house.

I loved them but one visit was enough.

I stayed the summer in the old house.

It was a very small bungalow, built by people who had no plans for luxury on very limited resources. I would guess it was no more than 24 x24 with a woodshed attached out back.

There was a big room that served as the Living Room/Dining room. A wood stove on the west side of the room that heated the house and two very small bedrooms that had doorways that instead of doors had curtains that you opened and drew back depending on the situation (needed privacy/ needed heat).

I loved the place.

I would go down to the creek below the house and catch two or three brook trout then have them for supper. Aunt Beatrice had taught me long before to clean them, roll them in flour and spices and cook them in butter, lard or bacon fat.

The water supply was a 3 foot hole in the ground on the other side of the property about 20 feet from the house. This was an artesian well that brought up water from deep in the earth. It was covered by a square board. If you dipped a cup in the well to take a drink the water was so cold it could pop the fillings in your teeth. It was just large enough to dip a large metal pail to fill with drinking water.

I used the Creek water for washing and bathing.

There was no refrigerators in Grandma's old house. But there was a Root Cellar right under the house. Because the house was built on a 45 degree angle slope, so the front and sides were supported with a stone and concrete wall. There was one door into the cellar on the east side. Inside it was cool and damp with a dirt floor. Shelves were on every wall except one were Grandma and my Aunt used to store extra firewood.

It was in this root house that I kept my milk and eggs and food supplies.

By the end of summer my Dad was still in a foul mood, so my Mother asked me would I like to go to Grade 11 in Denbigh? I was all for it. S got a transcript of my Grade 9 and 10 marks from Ottawa Tech a them to the School Board. I was now 16 and allowed to live at that age.

School was much different in Denbigh. The other boys and girls were much more friendly and easy going than Ottawa kids. I was a bit of a novelty as rumour had it that my mother was a rich Landlord with lots of money and her kid Leslie had an unlimited supply of cash. Little did they know.

Sometimes my $10 per week never arrived. I'd write my Mom a letter (no phone, all I could afford) and ask her why she skipped my grocery money. She would write back that she had sent it and didn't understand why I'd never received it.

I later found out that the person in town with the Post Office was stealing money from the mails. It didn't take too much brains to figure out each week after I got my envelope from Ottawa I went right to the General Store and bought a bunch of groceries.

Since I wasn't the only one she was skimming she eventually got caught red-handed and lost the Post Office Contract. I don't know if there were any criminal charges laid.

The school principle and head teacher was Ezra Brown. He was very strict but very good in his subjects: English Literature, Composition, Geography and History (my favourite subjects!) The other teacher I couldn't stand. He was fresh out of teacher's college (his first teaching assignment) and teached my most hated subjects (Mathematics, Science, French and Physics).

I lived less than a mile from school in Grandma's old house. The rule back then was the school bus only picked you up if you lived more than a mile from school. So for the first few weeks of September, I walked the 9/10th of a mile to school and back. As it grew colder in October, the School Bus Driver took pity on me and suggested I walk down to the neighbour's gate which was just past the one mile mark. This was a few hundred yards from my place. Later in the fall, as it grew increasingly colder, The Bus Driver told me, never mind walking all the way down to that stop. Keep your eye on the road each morning: when you see me coming around the bend, you boot it out of the house straight down the hill and across the footbridge and meet me at the highway in front of your place. He would stop down the road, take on the kids at that stop then start up to where I was standing. I could hear him starting in first gear, shifting into second gear, then right away he slowed down to pick me up.

I made my supper every night on the hardwood stove. I ate cheap. Hot Dogs, Hamburgers, Bacon and Eggs, Fish from the creek.

I'd make a lunch to take to school. It could be baloney or peanut butter and jam. I also bought Klick and Kam (a meat sandwich spread). When I ran out of these, I'd fry an egg in the morning, put it in the sandwich after it cooled down and eat that at lunch. It was kind of greasy, but it went down smooth.

Later in life there was a T.V. Commercial where Kam (the beef spread) was talking to a can of Klik (the pork spread).

It went something like this:

"Say Moo…. OINK!"
" Say MOO!.... OINK!"
"SAY MOO!!...... "I can't, It's not in me!!"

A new problem developed. I didn't have hardly any firewood for the stove. The little firewood I had I used for cooking. There was a coal oil heater that I lit on really cold nights in my bedroom.

It just so happened that my Mom's boarder Robert Wilson was going up to Bancroft to visit his parents very early on a Saturday morning. He must have left Ottawa very early as he pulled into my road at 6:30 a.m. I was still asleep but woke up quick when walked into the house and shouted: **" Holy Shit, Leslie! What happened in here?"**

During the night, while was I was sound asleep, the coal oil heater malfunctioned and spewed black soot all over the bedroom and into the main house. Even my face was black and I looked like a young male version of Aunt Jemima. The two bedrooms in the house didn't have doors, just narrow curtains that you pulled shut when you retired or were changing your clothes.

My curtain was now black as tar.

Robert said maybe we should start thinking about other arrangements… you're running out of firewood and the coal oil heater is history.

Robert returned to Ottawa that Sunday night and explained what had happened. My mother came up with the idea that maybe I should room and Board right in Denbigh. So the next time I was in the General Store I asked the owner if there was anyone who took in Boarders in the village. He said he'd get back to me.

About a week later he said, go see Mrs. Fritz. She lives in the house at the corner of the hill, the white house with the green roof. So I stopped in and introduced myself. She drilled me with questions about my parents, school, my hobbies and finally stated she'd take me in for $60 per month room & board.

****

I wrote my mother a letter explaining the deal (no phones back in those days) and about a week later I got a letter with a $60 money order payable to Mrs. Fritz. (No longer sending cash in the mail).

This was a big change from my independence 9/10th of a mile down the road. Mrs. Fritz had two pre-teen daughters that I got along with from the first day. Mrs. Sandra Fritz was a very attractive lady in her early thirties. Her daughters were both very pretty young girls and very outgoing.

Right from the start I hit it off with Veronica and Elizabeth as they loved poetry and literature. So a routine was established quite early that after supper each night I would read them a story or a poem. It would be from one of their books from school or something I would choose that I thought fit their pre-high school level.

Mrs. Fritz sometimes exercised on the rug in the living room. She would be wearing either leotards or shorts. It was quite the sight for a 13 year old boy and was a source of many erotic fantasies about my Landlord.

Her husband worked in the mines in Sudbury and only came home once a month. The first time he came home I received a very cool reception. I heard them arguing late at night when everyone was supposed to be asleep and I figured my days there were numbered.

Sure enough, after Mr. Fritz left for the mines in Sudbury, Sandra sat me down for a talk. She told me I better start looking for another place to stay as her husband didn't want me in the same house as his two pretty young daughters. He didn't trust me. I asked her if I had ever done anything to Veronica or Elizabeth to suggest there was a problem. She said: **"It's not you Leslie, He's just over protective and very territorial".**

After I thought about it for a while I figured out that he was just plain jealous and was worried I was a horny young teenage boy who was going to try to take a run at his wife some night.

****

There was an old couple that lived next door to my Grandma's place. Walter and Hazel Schultz. They were in their 70's but were always very friendly to me. One day I walked down from the village and propositioned them for the room and board deal. I told them, besides the $60 per month I'd do chores for them: bring in firewood, feed the chickens, gather the eggs, split firewood. They agreed on the spot and I moved in the next week.

This was different from anything I ever experienced. Again no Hydro, no running water, an outhouse out back. You went to sleep each night with many blankets and comforters as the house dropped to below zero every night in the winter. In the morning old Walter would get up and start a fire in the woodstove. By then the metal dish full of water on the top of the stove had frozen over. This melted real quick once the fire started.

One day old Walter was very disturbed and asked me to do him a favour. He said **"See that godamned chicken hawk circling up there in the sky?"**

I looked up and sure enough there was the chicken hawk.

Walter said: **"He's already killed two of my chickens and I can't hold the gun steady anymore, I shake too much. Would you try to shoot him for me?"**

So he went into the house and brought out this WW2 303 calibre Lee Enfield. The bullets I noticed were as long as my middle finger.

Walter said: **"These are not the standard copper jackets, these have mushroom tips, if you hit him, he'll explode"** as he loaded the gun with 3 bullets.

So I tried shooting with the gun standing up. The recoil was hard on my shoulder and I missed completely. I decided to lay down on the sandbank and hold the gun very tight to my shoulder. My second shot blew a few feathers of the hawk. But now I realized I had to move ahead of his curved flight so he would fly into the bullet. Not much, just about six inches ahead of him. The next bullet was the big one. There was an explosion of feathers and blood and the hawk (what was left of him) dropped out of the sky like a stone.

Walter and Hazel were delighted and cooked my favourite dinner that night. Hot Hamburg sandwich with Brown Gravy.

Hazel had a couple of pet zingers. One would be if someone started a sentence with the word "Well". She would break in immediately and ask:" **How many wells does it take to make a river?"** The other person would say," **I don't know, how many?"** To which Hazel would respond: **"Two or three as shallow as you!"** followed by a loud chuckle.

Another one she got me on one day when I'd mentioned that I was born in Ottawa, to which she said: **"You weren't born."** I said:"What?" She chuckled and said," **You weren't born. The crows came along and shyte you on a rock and the sun hatched you out!"** (She never said shit with the soft "I").

I now had my next great romantic experience. There was a girl in grade 9 Loretta Stein that I couldn't take my eyes off. She was a fully developed age 13 and had shining brown hair and dark brown eyes. A typical German descent fraulein. She became interested in me much to my astonishment and we would take walks down the road from the school so we could be together and have talks before her school bus came along.

On one of these walks I escorted her into the bush beside the road and kissed her. She didn't resist and kissed me back. Just then the school bus came along and she ran out and flagged it down.

I was mesmerized. I decided she was the one and only. Forget that heartbreaker in Ottawa, Brittany Hillis. She was a dog compared to Loretta. But my heart was to be broken yet again.

After a while it became clear to everyone in this village that not only was I not rich, but I was in fact poor if not poverty stricken. Loretta clued into this real quick and all of a sudden I was backtracked to Jason McKenny, a spoiled brat only son of a resort owner 20 miles down highway 41. He was 16 had his license and the use of Daddy's station wagon on the weekends. He was also the best dressed kid in school sporting a red Leather jacket and different coloured expensive slacks every day.

One day before I'd moved out from the Fritz's house Loretta showed up. She started the conversation by requesting I give back the picture of herself that she had given me and I carried in my wallet. She said: **"It's over Leslie, I'm going steady now with Jason and I want my picture back."**

I said:" **Fine, no problem, have a nice life**" and fished the picture out of my wallet and handed it to her.

About a week later her new boyfriend confronted me in the school yard in front a large audience and said in a loud voice **"Just stay away from Loretta or I'll kick the shit out of you."**

My response was: **"Now that she's been with you, I wouldn't touch her with a ten foot pole!"**

The year flew by but somewhere in the winter I met up with Chuck Fritz. He was an exceptional guitar player and singer. He was a nephew to my original next door neighbours and current landlords Walter and Hazel and always had his guitar with him every where he went. I had bought a guitar in Vars one night for $10 but while I tried to play it I just wasn't catching on. Chuck took me under his wing and started to teach me chords, change-ups and bass runs.

Soon I had a new hobby. Every night, I'd practice my chords. I sat beside the radio and the coal oil lamp and if I heard a song I liked I'd write down the words as fast as I could as the song played. Sometimes it took two or three listenings to get all the right words in the right places on the lines.

Then I'd practice the song. I had to experiment with the chords until I figured it out. Usually not a problem as most song chords back then were mostly G.C.D.

The year ran itself out and I returned back to Ottawa. I had stolen 3rd place in marks. There was a girl who was unbeatable 90% grade average, then my rival Garry Plotz, an 88% average, I pulled in at 86% beating out his girlfriend (who had always been # 3 for years). She ended up at 85% average.

Before I left I became fascinated with Public Toilet graffiti. There are two kinds of Graffiti. There's the disgusting stuff and the more inventive inscriptions. At the Municipal Hall there were outside toilet's, Men's and Ladies. In the Men's somebody with a poetic nature had scrolled in pen on the stall wall:

"A person's mind must be pretty small.
To write his sayings on a shithouse wall"

In the next lantrine, I think the same author wrote:

"Some people come here to sit and think,
I come here to shit and stink!"

Down the road on Highway 41 there was a restaurant that had an indoor toilet.

Inside the bathroom there was a sign on the wall:

"If it's yellow, let it mellow,
If it's brown, flush it down.. "

Later on in life in Ottawa I was a regular at the YMCA near Catherine Street. They had installed "pay toilet's". You had to insert a dime to get into the toilet and relieve yourself. In one of the toilet's someone had written on the wall:

"Here I sit broken hearted,
Paid a dime and only farted!"

Later in life I was in a hotel on Eddy Street in Hull. In the men's room someone had gotten up on a step ladder and wrote on the ceiling about six feet from the wall:

"if you can read this you're probably pissing on the floor.."

Chapter 8.

Back to Ottawa...

My Dad had mellowed out by now. My mother had this thing in her mind that I should take Grade 12 at Ottawa U High School on Main Street. It was run by the priests. I didn't last there 3 weeks. I couldn't stand the attitude of the priests and went into Ottawa Tech and applied for Grade 12 there. With my grade average from Denbigh they accepted me on the spot.

School went well except for Math and French which I both failed by 49% and 48%. I never got along with my Math teacher or my French teacher. I think they were trying to send me a message. All my other subjects ranged from 70% to high 90's.

I made through until June and that final eventful day when you walked out of high school on the last day graduated (or semi-graduated in my case).

I was informed that I needed to repeat both Math and French before I'd be allowed into Grade 13.

Yeah, Right.

As I sailed out that back door of Ottawa Tech, I remembered back in Grade School when the last day of school came we all had chanted:

**"No more pencils, No more books,
No more teacher's dirty looks!"**

That was it for me and school. Now I was going to join the working class.....

Chapter 8.

Leslie gets a job.

Back then the Unemployment Insurance Office (U.I.C.) was Slater Street, right next door to Ottawa Tech. Some people told me I should go and register and see what jobs were available. Other people told me get a newspaper and find your own job, the people at U.I.C. are useless.

I went in to the U.I.C. building. I was told, I just finished High School but had no experience in the work world. I looked at the job postings and everything required a degree of experience, so I went and bought the Ottawa Citizen and the Ottawa Journal.

Since I always had a burning desire to join the RCMP since a very young age I went to the RCMP recruiting office at "N" Division in Rockliffe. I marched in to the recruiting office and announced that I was there to apply for the job. The recruiting Officer told me before I could write any written tests I needed to pass certain minimum physical standards. I had to be at least five foot eight inches tall and they would measure my chest, apply a formula and determine if I qualified. No problem with the height: I was five feet eight and a half inches. Then they measured my chest size at full expansion and breath fully expired. They added the two numbers together and informed me I was 3 inches short of the minimum required. "Sorry kid".

My dreams to become a Mountie went up in smoke.

Onward and forever upward.

I saw an ad in the Journal for a sales person at Bata shoe store in Carlingwood Shopping Centre. Base salary plus commission.

I went out the next day and walked right into the store and asked for the Manager. He came out from the back and I introduced myself. We seemed to hit it off from the start and he told me that he'd try me out on a probationary basis for a month. If I made the grade, he'd hire me full-time.

The deal would be $37.50 per week plus commission. I had to work Friday nights until nine p.m. and Saturdays 9:00 a.m. until 6:00 p.m. I could get a morning off or afternoon during the week to make sure I didn't exceed 40 hours per week.

I asked how did I earn commission? The boss explained that I was paid the $37.50 for selling all the easy merchandise. Then they had "spiffs". I asked what was a spiff. He advised that this is a pair of shoes, women's, men's, children's or could be slippers, boots, running shoes that had sat on the shelves too long. If you sell them you get a bonus on your pay. The more you sell the more you boost your pay. If a spiff had one red star on it, you got an extra commission, two stars got you double and three stars got you triple.

I soon learned that these so called spiffs were the ugliest footwear in the store. But they had to be unloaded to make room for faster moving merchandise and at the same time line Leslie's pockets with money!!

I couldn't imagine how shoe designers could come up with some of their creations. And it was mostly in women's shoes. Some would have pointy toes that I referred to as "toad stabbers". Some had ridiculously high heels, others with gaudy brass or silver buckles that really cheapened the shoe in my opinion.

The men's shoes weren't as bad but there were some loafers that no one in their right mind would walk around town in.

But I was amazed to find out that there are certain ladies that require lots of shoes. Any shoes. It was like they were filling a void in their life. Maybe they just needed to get out of the house and visit Carlingwood Mall and have a nice 18 year old well dressed young man take off their shoe and try on several new shoes.

In any event, they would ask which shoe I'd recommend. Of, course it was always the spiff! **" It suits you to a "T" Madame!"** I would say. Then we'd go up to the cash and I'd talk her into buying some Tana shoe polish. (got commission on that, too!!)

When I first started there there was an Assistant Manager, Kevin Schultz. His Dad owned a very successful hardware store in Smith's Falls but somewhere along the line he and Dad had a falling out so he was working in the Bata Shoe store in Ottawa just to get even or punish his Dad.

He was very handsome, tall, well dressed, much better than an employee in a shoe store would dress. I felt like a second class citizen the way I could afford to dress compared to him. Then there was his girlfriend. She worked in the Simpson's Sears Store and was a knockout. Everytime she came into the store, every eye was turned on her. She was an earlier version of Farrah Fawcett Majors.

After I worked there a few months I got brave and walked into the E.R.Fisher Men's Clothing store. This was a men's store that sold better clothes than you could buy at Sears but at a larger price tag. I decided I wanted to raise my clothing bar up to the same standards as our handsome Assistant Manager.

The owner of the store took me aside and suggested I needed to upgrade my wardrobe. I told him I'd like to do that but could I pick something out and put it on layaway, I could put $10 down today.

He took me to the suit rack and picked out a Grey Herringbone 3 piece suit that fit me to a "T". I was in love with the suit and said I'll take it, can you put it away for me. He said: **"Why don't you take it home, I'll open you a charge account"**.

Since I didn't have a clue what a charge account was I asked him: **"How does that work?"**

He explained that all I had to do was pay them $20 per month until the bill was paid. Before I left he made sure I had a new brand name long sleeve shirt and a silk tie that matched the suit. The next day I came to work in my new outfit and all the employees were very impressed. That was the fall. I had the suit paid off by the spring. When I made my final payment on the suit, the Manager of the store asked me if I intended to wear that Herringbone suit all year round?

The next thing you now he was introducing me to an "ultra-light" "summer-weight" blue-ish, green-ish, turquoise-ish 2 piece suit. So I re-opened my charge account with of course a new summer shirt and matching tie.

In the summer a girl from the Carling avenue area was hanging around the mall.

Tanya Stalkie. She was about 16 and stunningly beautiful. We struck up a conversation and before you knew we were dating. Our first date was to go to "Le Hibou" a very campy coffee house on Bank Street. They served up expresso and lots of folk music.

Originally Le Hibou had started up in a small upstairs apartment at 544 Rideau Street. They later moved to 248 Bank Street in a larger room upstairs from a storefront business. There was a long flight of stairs up to the coffee house but you walked through the door into a great atmosphere. The ultimate Getaway.

It was that time when folk music was coming on strong. Peter Paul &Mary, Bob Dylan, Joan Baez, Pete Seeger, Gord Lightfoot.

A great deal of talent performed on that stage in it's early years. Canadians such as Gord Lightfoot, Neil Young, Buffy Ste-Marie and Murray McLaughlin had shown their stuff. We even attracted such noted artists from the States such as John Prine, T Bone Walker and Odetta.

By this time I was a regular attendee at this coffee house. I never missed a Tuesday night Talent night and practiced all the latest folk songs that were the rage at the time. I was impressed with the nice guitars the performers had ranging from Martins, Gibson's, Guild and Fender. I saved up my money and bought the newest out on the market at Blue Note Music on Sparks Street. It was a Gibson 12 String model B25 12 N. I got it and the case for around $200. If I had any brains I would never have parted with it, as it was one of the first off the line and these days would be worth thousands.

The first night I showed up with it at Le HiBou I got a lot of attention. One of the main entertainers there was Bruce Hodgins. He later adopted the stage name of "Sneezy Rivers" and made several records and even appeared in some movies.

He really liked my Gibson and asked if he could play it on one of his sets that night. I said, **"I'll make you a deal. I'll lend you the Gibson if you teach me the chords and bass runs and the words to San Francisco Bay Blues!"**

He agreed. The next day I would go to Le Hibou early before the crowds started and he'd teach me what was his signature song at the time. This was a song written by Woody Guthrie in the late 30's during the Great Depression. Guthrie also wrote This Land is Your Land and many other famous songs.

It was a song that was particularly suited to a twelve string guitar.

There was only one other twelve string player at this hangout. He was an Albino from Renfrew Ontario. He always wore sunglasses (just like Roy Orbison) but his hair was pure white even though he was in his early 20's. He had a terrific voice. He would belt out Kingston Trio and Peter Paul and Mary songs that were excellent renditions. My favourite of his on the 12 string was "Green Green, It's Green they say on the far side of the hill".

Neville Wells was up on talent nights as well as Bruce Cockburn and Colleen Peterson. On talent night I would get up and play sometimes before and sometimes after Bruce Cockburn. At the time I thought he was not a big deal and he was wasting his time getting up on stage. Little did I know.

Somebody taught me a really short folk song that was made for the twelve string guitar.

It went something like this:

I got and old Tom Cat,
And when he steps out.
All the cats in the neighbourhood,
They begin to shout,

And they say:
Here comes ring-tailed Tom
Struttin' round the town,
If you got your heat turned up,
You better turn your damper down!"

But back to my first(and only) date with Tanya.

We went there one night and took in the sights and scenes for a while and then she said let's get out of here, I want to listen to some good old rock and roll. I invited her to my place and told her I had lots of 45 rpm's of the best.

We went to my apartment. Mom and Dad were sound asleep and we snuck up to my bedroom. After a few tunes on the phonograph and some hot kisses we started to undress each other. You know the rest. When you're a 19 year old young man with a beautiful 17 year old young woman the hormones kick in and take over.

About two months later she met me outside the store and informed me she was three months pregnant and in "deep shit" with her parents.

She too, like me had been adopted at an earlier age but never seemed to fit into or be accepted by her upper crust family. Before I'd met her she had even won a competition as a teen model and had been featured in Chatelaine doing a full page commercial for Tampons.

But she was beside herself and told me: **"You're not the father Leslie it's that Italian prick at the Carlingwood Restaurant. When I told him I was pregnant he said "Take a hike" and now I'm screwed!"**

"My parents want me to get an abortion, but I'm not into that. Number one it can screw me up so I never have kids again and I don't believe in killing an unborn child."

I was totally devasted. I was very confused, half-assed in love with her, but at that age not really having a clue about what I should do. I threw any amount of wisdom out the window and said : **"Tanya we'll get an apartment I'll take care of you, after you can't work, I'll take care of you and the baby."**

She was a lot smarter than me. She said: **"You don't love me Leslie… you just got a hard on for me."**

"I'll do this on my own. Thanks for being such a good friend and I'll call you if I need you."

A few month's later she called me. She was about 8 month's along and needed some money to help pay her rent. She was living in a ground floor flat on Arlington Street. She was very round in the belly and had a lot of pimples on her face. After I gave her the cash she said: **"This is not the place for you, man, better go."**

She said she'd get back to me after she had the kid. Never did.

After that I made a major stupid mistake. I had fallen out of love with folk music and into love with Rock and Roll. I took my 12 string Gibson and traded it in for an Electric Guitar and Amplifier. I wanted to play Chuck Berry and Johnny Rivers and Elvis songs now. If I'd held onto that original 12 string Gibson years later it would be worth a fortune.

I somehow got a gig at the Chez Henri Hotel in Hull on Principale Street. I was going to be the opening act for Hank Lariviere, of local fame.

I got up and did my songs: Maybelline, Johnny Be Good, Memphis Tennissee, Blue Suede Shoes.

Then in came Hank Lariviere and his girl friend. He thanked me for warming up the audience and then said I'll buy you all the Zombies you can drink here if you can drink more than two! I took his bet.

The next thing I remember was waking up in my bed in Ottawa. My guitar and Amp were beside my bed and a handwritten note by Hank or his girlfriend: "Leslie, you better stay away from Zombies, ha ha!"

****

Back at the shoe store, I had never been allowed to fit children's shoe's. It was either the Boss or the Assistant Manager. But I was allowed to sit in on every child's shoe fitting to learn. I also was allowed to assist in the window displays.

Before you know it, I was allowed to fit Children's shoes. This was about the same time Kevin Schultz tendered his resignation as Assistant Manager and I was promoted to the job. No raise in pay, just a new title.

Meanwhile my love life just gets into the tank again.

There was this German girl and her sister that both worked in the mall. Jutta was the older sister (my age) a beautiful brunette with the typical high cheekbones and all the rest of the right equipment. We dated once then she latched on to an executive type man with a sports car and expensive suits. She didn't need a relationship with a shoe salesman.

Her sister Bronwen was another thing altogether. Blonde hair, blue eyes, the high cheek bones, she was a beauty. Only 17 and looking for a boyfriend. We went out on a date and she figured out I wasn't the executive type her sister had snared so on the last date, I took her home in a cab, kissed her goodnight as she got out of the cab she said :" **I don't think you and I have a future together, Lesie."**

So I said to the cabbie: **"I guess I'm wasting my time with that gal!"**

And I said: **"I'm from Lebreton Flats, she's looking for a Rockliffe Park, Island Park kind of guy, not me…"**

The cabby said (an older guy with white hair talking to an 18 year old fare) **"Sometimes you are just end up being a small fish in a big pond"**…

I decided it was time to get some transportation. My Dad and I went to Campbell Ford, the only place he'd deal with. They had a red VW Beetle just traded in and the salesman said that didn't like them "furrin' jobbies" on the lot and we could buy it cheap. They'd even arrange the financing through TCC (Trans Canada Credit). But my Dad had to co-sign for me. The payments were cheap $50 per month. I didn't need insurance back then, all you needed was an Ontario Government thing called "Proof of Financial Responsibility". It was a $100 add on to the price of the car, and you needed it to transfer the ownership. Without it you needed real car insurance. At my age, I couldn't afford real Insurance.

Things went well at first. I rodded all over town in my bug. Then I got the bright idea to go into business "on the side," a weekend enterprise. I would sell Watkins products. They sold spices, lotions, medications, farm products, instant beverages and cleaning products.

I sold some in town to friends and relatives and started to get over confident. I decided I'd head on up to Denbigh and sell all my relatives, old school mates and the local farmers that I knew.

Just outside of Dacre, it started to snow heavily. It was a blizzard, with swirling snow squalls and zero visability. I cut my speed in half, but coming around one corner saw what I thought was a wolf or a dog in the middle of the road. I hit the brakes and lost it completely. The VW started into 360 degree spins and before I knew it I had crossed the road and plunged backwards into a ditch crashing into an old split rail fence. I had bumped my head on the steering wheel and blacked out for a while.

When I awoke, I realized my predicament and was starting to panic when a local person from Dacre discovered me and stopped. He took me into Dacre to his place and called the Renfrew OPP. They came and got me and the VW was towed to Renfrew. It survived the crash well, just needed the hood over the engine bended back into shape and away she went no problem.

But my red VW was on marked time. I got it back to Ottawa and the very next week I was cruising down Carling Avenue just before the entrance to Westgate Shopping Centre. An OTC (Ottawa Transportation Commission) bus was pulling out of Westgate on a green light. My light was red. I hit the brakes. Carling Avenue was a combination of ice, snow and freezing rain. I slid non-stop into the bus. The VW was a total write off. I ended up selling it to someone for $50 for parts. But I never missed a payment at Trans Canada Credit for the next three years. I didn't dare.

Three years later when I made the last payment on the VW I brought the paid promissory note and loan contract home, handed it to my Dad and said: "I'll never ask you to sign for me again, Dad. If I can't get it on my own. I'll do without…."

Chapter 9.

The next stage...

Just about this time my Mom took in a new boarder. Our Mountie decided he wanted to rent one of the apartments in our building with another Mountie he was in training with and had befriended.

The new boarder was quite different. At first glance you would have thought he was my older brother. He was the Manager of Beneficial Finance on Bank Street.

He was twenty one and I was nineteen. We became close friends from day one.

He had an easy name to remember. Jack Wilson. He later explained to me that he changed his name to a familiar Canadian name because his birth name from Estonia where his parents escaped from in the Soviet Block was a big long unpronounceable name for the average Canadian,.

Before you knew it he was taking me up to his office when he'd work late at night doing his collection calls to delinquent customers. He'd even take me out on repossession calls to clients that weren't making their payments on TV's, stereos and cars.

We actually became like brothers. He told me one night he had a sister but always wanted a brother and the rest was history. The next thing you know he bought a 1962 Plymouth Valiant Convertible. We drove all over Ottawa and Aylmer and Hull in this chick magnet machine. He was introducing me to the nightlife in our area. We'd go to the Interprovincial Hotel in Hull and drink Beer and listen to the music of the day. The favourite song on the jukebox at the Interprovincial was" You've lost that lovin' feeling" by the Righteous Brothers.

He later traded in the Valiant for a Dodge Savoy. It was the ugliest car I'd ever seen in my life. It had a big chrome grille like almost a grinning shark, had these two rocket taillights at the back and was utterly devoid of design or "chick magnetism".

I asked him why did you buy this car? He said come with me. He popped the hood and said: " You see that engine? That's a 426 Hemi. Now get in the car."

The 426 Hemi was just recently out by Chrysler Corporation. "Hemisphere Combustion Engine". Soon to win many drag races and professional races all across the North American Continent.

"You see that speedometer? That's a cop speedometer. This was an OPP Interceptor. See that push button Automatic? Wait'll you see this sucker go!!"

So go we went. One day we were on Carling avenue at the same intersection as Turpin Pontiac Buick. We had the red light.

While we were waiting for green a newer model Dodge 440 Sport pulled up beside us. Obviously the Dad's car, son out for a spin with his teenage buddies. They were grinning at Jack and revving that Dodge 440. **WANTA RACE??** Said the fool.

Jack said: **"I been waiting for this day. Sit back in your seat, man we're gonna smoke these suckers, I'm only gonna need First gear!"**

At that point the light turned green and he hit the push button marked number one and put the accelerator to the floor. The Savoy took off sideways with screeching and smoking tires then took off like a rocket leaving the Dodge 440 way behind. He laughed and I said : (typical Ottawa Valley expression I'd learned over the years) **"Sure showed them where the bear shit in the Buckwheat!"**

The next thing you know Jack got this thing for going to New York State to the bars. He liked American Beer especially Budweiser on Draft.

His favourite destination was Watertown, New York. There was a bar there that he really liked the atmosphere and we were there every weekend. I remember the most popular song on the juke box (and the car radio) was " The House of the Rising Sun" by the Animals.

One night we were in that Bar and he was drinking a lot heavier than usual. He kept saying that he'd had a really rough week at work and wanted to get it out of his system. I kept telling him he was drinking too much and how were we going to get back home?

He threw me the keys and said: **"You drive, Man"**. Shortly after that he passed out.

I got the Bartender to help me carry him out and load him into the car in the passenger seat. We left and crossed over at Custom's. At Canadian Custom's all they asked was how was my chum? I said he's had a rough week at work and needs his sleep. They motioned us on through.

About halfway to Kemptville from the Bridge to the USA on the way back to Ottawa I crested this hill doing about 100 miles an hour. On the other side of the hill there was an accident in progress. Two cars had just collided and were separating and headed for their respective ditches. I had only a hope and a prayer to get through the space that was available after they collided and started to part company.

It was a miracle but I threaded the needle and made it through the two spinning off vehicles.

I woke up Jack and said**:" Hey man, we just came through a major accident!"**

I described what we just went through and he said, keep going, the first gas station we come to we'll report it but we're in deep shit if we hang around.

As we breezed through the next town we noticed cop cars and an ambulance passing us. Somehow or other they were alerted to the problem, maybe a passerby with a CB radio.

We had intended to call in on a payphone but it turned out unnecessary no one was hurt, just shaken up having landed in snowdrifts in the ditches.

Chapter 10:
The Credit business…

That was when Jack started to encourage me to get into the Consumer Credit Industry. He insisted I could do well. He couldn't hire me at Beneficial because he was already at full staff.

I was getting fed up with the shoe business and I was reading the want ads every night. Soon there was an ad for Citizen's Finance on Richmond Road in Westboro. They were looking for a "Credit Trainee".

It paid $45.00 per week. I applied and was hired.

The Manager, Bill Knight was a very sleazy type person. He wore shiny polyester suits and never had his tie pulled up to his collar. He also smelled of BO. He was originally from the USA where he had a lot of experience working in HFC and other small Finance company operations around Ohio and New York State. The Assistant Manager Brad Wollum was a real good person, always dressed neatly, was nice to the customers and staff and the only reason I stuck around.

Then there were multiple back to back experiences that I survived but just barely.

We had a company car. It was a blue Volkswagen Beetle. The Manager didn't like me much. I wasn't hardened enough to suit him.

One of my first assignments was to go and get a Wage Assignment from a delinquent customer. He had phoned in and told the Manager he was back to work and would pay him so much per pay until he got caught back up. The Manager told him that would be OK but he'd have to sign a Wage Assignment in case he defaulted. Back then Finance companies could use this which was like a voluntary wage Garnishee for 33% of your wages.

So I went to this man's home which was an apartment in Lowertown. (Lowertown was anything back then on the north side of Rideau Street after Sussex).

He was a huge black man married to a small Chinese lady. They had three small girls ranging from three to eight years old, all beautiful kids. We had a great visit and I got the Wage Assignment signed.

When I got back to the office, the Manager told me to mail it to the customer's pay office. But I said: **"You made a deal with him to accept so much per pay!!"**

"To hell with the deal, he's so far behind he'll never catch up. My job is to collect this shit!!"

The next day he sent me out on two collection calls one in Gatineau the other in Pointe Gatineau.

The one in Gatineau didn't go well. As soon as I identified myself as an employee of Citizen's Finance looking for a payment the lady cursed at me in French and slammed the door in my face.

I went to a payphone and called into the office to report my lack of progress on that double write-off file. The Manager told me that the lady in Gatineau had called in after my visit and said to him **"If that little bastard in the blue Volkswagen ever comes here again, I've got a 12 guage Shotgun loaded with rock salt and I'll nail him and that VW with both barrels!"**

My boss thought that was real funny and let out a hearty guffaw. I wasn't enjoying the humour one bit. Then he seals the conversation with: **"Don't forget your collection call on those Ouellette deadbeats in Pointe Gatineau."**

This one turned out to be the deal breaker in my short lived career in the Finance Company business.

At first everything went well. I pulled into the Ouellette's laneway. They lived in a rundown shack neat the Gatineau River. There was garbage and junk and old rusted cars laying around their yard. I introduced myself to Mrs. Ouellette and surprisingly enough she was quite friendly and invited me in. I explained I was there to collect a payment on their loan which was six month's overdue (actually a triple write off!)

She told me she had just received her welfare cheque that day and would I mind driving her to the Pointe Gatineau IGA so she could cash her cheque and buy her groceries. Then she could give me $20 out of her cheque as a payment. I was fine with that as at least I'd get back to the office with a positive result from my trip to Quebec.

We went to the IGA and loaded up with groceries, I carried most of them to the car, then from the car into the house. She handed me the $20. Everything was going great. I pulled out a duplicate receipt book and started to write her out a receipt.

That's when as they say: "the shit hit the fan!"

In walked Mr. Ouellette having spent half the day in the local tavern and half in the bag. He looked at me, then his wife and the conversation began in Pointe Gatineau French (which I understood completely). Here's the English version:

" **Who's this little prick, Jeanne D'Arc and what's he doing here?**"
"**He's from Citizen's Finance Jean and he was nice enough to take me to the store to get our groceries so I'm giving him a little payment on your loan.**"

"**Bullshit! No way! I'm not giving them assholes a dime!**"

Then he turned to me with a look of absolute rage in his eyes and shouted: "**Give back that money or I'll kick the shit out of you!**"

At this point I decided discretion was the better part of valour. I threw my unfinished receipt in my briefcase, slammed it shut, threw the $20 bill at him and sprinted for the door then all the way to my VW as fast as my legs could travel.

As I climbed into the car I saw him coming through the door cursing me in a loud voice and running for the car. The engine started, thank God, and I slammed it in first gear and spun out the yard in a cloud of dust and gravel. I didn't slow down until I was crossing the Chaudiere Bridge.

The same day I resigned from Citizen's Finance Company. The Assistant Manager Brad tried to discourage me from quitting, but I was adamant. He told me that "things were coming down the pike" and "maybe you should stick around".

The truth were to be known, The Manager, Bill Knight had escaped from the USA with multiple fraud charges against him by his former employers. Citizen's hadn't done proper background checks on him as they needed a Manager in our Branch desperately. While he was there he was pocketing cash payments, giving the clients receipts, but never crediting their loans. In addition, he made phony loans to fictitious customers whose names and addresses he picked out of the Ottawa phone book.

Brad had his suspicions and even documented proof and reported to Head Office. Mr. Night I guess had a sixth sense about imminent danger and went to lunch just before Head Office security and Inspectors arrived, never to return.

So Brad became the new Manager and had to do double duty, since I decided not to stick around and fill his former position.

That week I scoured the Newspapers. There was an advertisement for "Credit Collection Trainees" at Interprovincial Collection Agency on Rideau Street.

I had told my buddy Jack about the ad and he said: **"Good place to learn collection procedures, Leslie… Go there learn the basics then get back into lending at a Bank, Finance or Acceptance company!"**

They paid less than Citizen's finance as a base salary, but much better than Bata on commission as you got much bigger commissions based on the value of the account, not like a $10 shoe.

Chapter 11,
The collection Agency

It wasn't long before I clued into how this job went and was picking up much better dollars than my previous jobs. I would make double my previous income easily.

Soon after I made the grade as full-time collector, they hired a new recruit from Haley's Station, a fellow named Mitch Klein. He had previously worked for the Hydro but injured himself on the job, so this was a fill-in way to make money as he recuperated. He had a real "Ottawa Valley Accent" and we were instant buddies.

Sometimes he'd call up a collection client and threaten them that he would have to garnishee their wages. But with his accent it came out **"I'm gonna have to Garr-on shee you sir!!"**

He really had the Ottawa Valley twang. For example the word sandwich came out of him as "sang-gwitch" and he didn't wash his hands he "warshed" them. When he first met someone, the first words out of his mouth were: "Gidday!"

We'd all chuckle in the background.

I sat behind the company skip tracer. Her name was Alice Jenkins, a late 50's early 60's very eccentric woman who wore flowery old-fashioned dresses and wore her salt and pepper hair in severely pulled back style with a bun at the back. She always wore a different coloured hairnet over the bun. Everyday a new coloured hairnet.

She also had a bag of tricks that simply amazed me. To start with she had about a half a dozen voices she could use, whatever suited the occasion. Her Bible was the Ottawa City Directory. She would look up the debtor's previous addresses, then from the City Directory, she'd start calling his or her former next door neighbours. Sometimes she would be Mrs. Jones legal secretary at Nelligan, Nelligan and Power Law firm. She was trying her best to locate Joe Debtor as she had an estate in which he was a beneficiary but "Joe probably doesn't know his Uncle had died and left him money." After one or two calls, she'd either get an address or his new job details. At this point she'd hand the file over to the Supervisor who would put a stamp after her last entry on the collection card that either say: ISSUE WRIT or ISSUE GARNISHEE (if we already had judgement in Small Claims Court). Joe Debtor never got a phone call at this point as he was constantly on the move and earnestly trying to avoid payments of his debts.

One time she located a debtor in a remote area in Alberta. He lived down the Road from an RCMP detachment. She had some nerve. She placed a collect call to the debtor care of the RCMP detachment phone number. The receptionist answered the call and informed Alice that Mr. Debtor doesn't live here "This is the RCMP office". Alice would say that she knew that, but it was urgent that she speak with him on an important family matter. After some conversation, it was agreed they would send a squad car to his place and inform him that he was to receive an important call at the detachment office. 30 minutes later Alice would make the second collect call and the phone was turned over to Joe Debtor. She then handed the call over to a collector who took over from there.

Her favourite line after pulling off a tough one was: **"I can find anyone, even if they're hiding under a rock!!"**

When the bosses weren't looking we'd play games on the new recruits. I was the lead person because I could talk with various accents, almost unrecognizable. I could do French, Italian, Chinese and Pakistani. The new employee would leave to go to the washroom. We'd pick a card out of his bin and write down the name of someone he had just called and left a message for. We knew for example it was a Simpson's Sears account for $134.25 past due.

The new guy would return to his desk. The client was French. I would go on line 4 and dial the main line of the Collection Agency. With of course, a French accent. I would ask for the newbie collector by name. The call was transferred to Newbie. Everyone in the room was listening.

Newbie would answer the call, "**Hello Joe Newbie here, can I help you?**"

I said : "**Dis is da guy you call for dat goddamm Sears account dat I ain't gonna pay for dem bastairs!!**"

"Excuse me sir, but who am I talking to?"

I'm Jean-Pierre Vachon, on Caruthers Street.

At this point he'd fish with his cards and find Mr.Vachon's card and make his best pitch.

"**Mr.Vachon, you owe Simpson's Sears $134.25 and haven't paid your bill in over a year. If you don't make arrangements today, Sir, with me we will have to take further measures with you!**"

So I'd come back with: "**Furder Measures! Furder Measures! You come and take dis useless piece of crap I bought from Sears and stick it up yer ass for de furder measures!!**"

Then I came in with the zinger. This is the one everyone listening was waiting for. A newbie was never ready for this next burst from the angry collection client...

"**Hey listen you fokker! I know who you are! Yer dat liitle prick wid de red hair an you leave dat place every night at five, right, Asshole?**"

"Excuse me Sir, what are you trying to tell me?"

"**I'm tole you, maybe you get run down by a fass car on Rideau Street. Maybe you get da shit kicked out of you for givin' hard times to deceen personnes trying to pay der way and not get fokked by dem godamm Sears bastairs!!**"

At this point he'd hang up the phone and go running for the Supervisor, who knew right away he'd been initiated.

The Supervisor would come into the Collection room with everbody snickering (about 12 collectors) and say: "**Swartmann, Would please lay off the new recruits!!**"

Then we'd stop snickering and bust into laughter...

One thing I was not impressed with with this company was the way they handled their Human Resources policies. There was one collector that had been there about six months. He just couldn't cut the mustard. He was always at the bottom of the totem pole in terms of production (dollars collected) so he made the least money of any employee in the organization.

His Supervisor was a relative of the Management and not very supervisorial. He would allude to the fact that this particular employee wasn't producing enough and didn't he think he was wasting his time in this kind of business? Or you are getting very close to being terminated unless you increase your results on your files. Where I really lost respect was when one that fateful Friday night, instead of telling him he was fired, that cowardly Supervisor wrote on his paycheque: "Final Paycheque".

This poor fellow wasn't all that sharp and didn't clue into the meaning. He went and cashed his cheque and Monday morning showed up for work as usual. This was when the Supervisor had to explain what "Final Paycheque" meant.

I thought it was really unprofessional and vowed I'd find a better deal out there sooner than later.

I was still living at home paying room and board to Mom and Pop. A new bunch of tenants moved into Apartment 12, all brothers from down east in Nova Scotia. They were all four of them body builders and had excellent physiques. Great guys, very friendly and I made instant friends with them, especially Ritchie the one the same age as me. A bonus was he played the guitar and sang country down east and Celtic songs.

We were both paid weekly on Fridays. So began a weekly ritual. We would alternate each week. I'd buy the 40 ouncer of Bacardi's White Rum and Ritchie would buy 3 large bottles of Pepsi. Or vice versa.

The other three brothers were out the door right after supper Friday nights to see their dates or bar-hopping. We had the apartment all to ourselves. We'd set the bottle of Rum, two glasses and a bottle of Pepsi on the coffee table. Then we'd get out the guitars, tune them up and have an all night jam session (or until we ran out of Rum). By then we were well "in the bag" and ready for bed.

One night I remember he was doing his down east songs and I suggested we do "Duelling Tear Jerkers". This was were who could sing the saddest song and get the other guy (or yourself) all steamy eyed. He was all for it.

He was a big Hank Snow fan (Hank was from Nova Scotia) and he started out with "Old Shep". That's a tough one to follow, but I countered with "Ebony Eyes" by the Everlys. Not to be out done he came back with "Nobody's Child" another Hank Snow song. I countered with my own Hank song "Little Buddy". This went on for about an hour until we exhausted or repertoire of Tear Jerkers.

Then we'd do our favourite songs. He'd sing a down East like "Farewell to Nova Scotia" or "I's the by that builds the boat".

One night I hit his funny bone. I remembered this song I learned at Le Hibou, a folk music hangout I spent a lot of time at. It went like this (very fast tempo):

"I'm going downtown to get a jug of Brandy,
Gonna bring it back to Mandy, get her good and drunk and goosy,
Good and Drunk and Goosy all the time...
"Cause yer skillet's good and greasy, skillet's good and greasy,
Skillet's good and Greasy all the time, time, time!
Good and Greasy! Skillet's good and Greasy
Skillet's good and greasy all the time...
If you say so, I'll never work no more
"I'll lay around yer shanty all the time, time ,time
Lay around your shanty all the time..
"Cause yer skillet's.....

I had to stop there as Ritchie was splitting his sides laughing.

" Where the HELL did you ever learn that song?" he said.

I told him at Le Hibou, a coffee house where I hung out a lot.

"It must be an "X" rated coffee house, man, you be careful who you sing that song to" then he started laughing again.

After a few months we figured we had an act we should try out at some talent contests.

At the time, a very popular group was Mac Beattie and the Ottawa Valley Melodiers. We had read in the paper that they were playing all weekend at the Richmond Fair and they would have a local talent set each night where performers could get up and strut their stuff.

Neither of us had a car, but Ritchie's brother had a VW Karmann Ghia and he was down with the flu that Friday night. He threw Ritchie his keys and said: **"Bring it back in one piece Bro!"**

We were off to Richmond. We went into the arena where the band was playing with our guitars in our cases. It seemed like we were the only ones that were there for the talent portion. We stood on the edge of the crowd and listened to the Band play their first two sets. When they broke after the last set Mac Beattie said into the microphone: **"When we get back folks we'll see if there's any local talent that want to get up and perform for you. I see two lads over there in the corner with Guitar cases so let's get them up right after we take our pause for the cause!"**

This made us major nervous and by the time the Band got back on stage we were sweating bullets. But we were called up and we went and did two double part harmony songs that we'd practiced to death. The first was a Ray Price song: "Crazy Arms", the second and Everly Brothers Song " Wake up Little Suzy". We were glad to finish and were getting to exit the stage when Mac said, "These guys sing well together, let's hear them solo!!"

I had this sinking feeling in my stomach and I pointed to Ritchie and said: **"He's First!"**

Then I said to Ritchie: **"Sing farewell to Nova Scotia, you know that song backwards!"**

He said:**"OK Man"** and ripped into it. He got a major applause.

Then it was my turn. He said: **" Sing that Lefty Frizell song "Long Black Veil"** I love that song, man.

But Mac said: **"No let's not do that. We want to keep things upbeat. Give us something with a beat"**. I said: **"How about Tiger by the Tail?"** a popular Buck Owens song at the time.

Mac said: **"Go for it!"**

I sang it, Ritchie broke into the choruses with double part harmony and we noticed that the couples up dancing, some were singing along with us. That was a really enjoyable part of the night.

We exited the stage with a lot of applause and then stole out of the Hall and pointed the VW back to Ottawa.

That night Ritchie decided he was going to put together a band and start playing the hotels. I was the exact opposite. I decided it was OK to have music as a hobby, but I wouldn't give up my day job for it.

Around this time Ritchie made friends somehow with two English governesses that were working in those upperscale houses in Rockliffe. Someone had found out that we were entertainers of sorts and we started to get invited to their teenage parties.

This led to many weekends of entertaining these rich teenagers in their Rockliffe rec rooms.

I became acquainted with one of the British governesses and she was very attractive and had a thick cockney accent.

Soon we were dating. Our last date was when I took her to the Rideau Theatre to see the very first showing of the "Sound of Music" with Julie Andrews and Christopher Plummer.

Before the night was over, I realized that she was just cruising for a Canadian husband so she could then get her Canadian Citizenship.

After that date, I dropped her like a hot potato.

After Mitch Klein and I worked together for six months, we saw we were making decent paycheques so we went on a rampage one weekend and decided we'd get an apartment together, and each buy a car at Myers Motors on the same weekend. We looked up the want ads and found an Apartment building on Gilmour Street, one bedroom apartment, two single beds and postage stamp kitchen, same size bathroom with a huge living room for $100 per month. We signed on the spot.

Then we went to Myers Motors on Catherine Street. They had this huge lot with everything on it. I was torn between an Austin Healey Convertible and a '62 Mercury Monterey Convertible. Mitch said: **"Don't buy that foreign shit, when it breaks down it'll cost you a fortune in parts!" "Anyway that Ford is a damn good car and a hell of a lot cheaper to fix than that other sucker!"**

He only looked at one car. It was a '62 Chevy Biscayne with a 283 V8. **"That's my car, man!!"**

Meanwhile, my Merc convertible had a 351 4 barrel carb and I figured I could smoke him anytime, anywhere. Ford Motor Company built three engine blocks at that time for their 351 cubic inch engines. They were the Detroit, Cleveland and Windsor. If your model was a 351 "Modified" it had larger bored cylinders and produced more horsepower (400 hp) than the other two. Mine was a modified!

We took delivery of the two cars the following week. We had been approved by GMAC (General Motors Acceptance Corporation).

Then began the daily races to work and the parking tickets. Every morning we got up, had our coffee, showered and dressed and then we would do our daily ritual.

Mitch would get into his Chevy. I'd get into my Mercury. We'd roll down our windows and shout at each other: **"GENTLEMAN START YOUR ENGINES!!"**

We'd turn on the cars and rev the engines. Then we'd yell at each other: **" THREE, TWO, ONE!!!"**

After that it was screeching tires and radios turned up at full volume, smoke coming out of our tires as we took off racing each other all the way down to Rideau Street.

Amazingly he beat me more times than not with his 283 because I wasn't as brave as him on the corners.

Every morning we would pick the parking tickets off our windshields. We'd heave them in the back seat. Eventually we brought them into the apartment and first we taped them on the mirror of our dresser. Then we ran out of room. So we taped them on the fridge door. Then we taped them on the window in the bedroom that we never looked out of. Finally we tore them all down and had a bonfire with them in the Alley. Next came the summonses.

This was about the time that Mitch was fully healed and had been called back to the Hydro. He paid his last month's rent and we sadly parted company.

I ended paying the summonses for my car and told them that Mitch had died in a car accident. I don't know if they accepted my story, but this gave rise to a new plan.

Mitch and I had subscribed unwittingly to "Columbia Records Club". You got a certain number of albums for a ridiculously low price if you became a member of the club. We both signed up and got a box of record albums each. They would mail you a new notice every month about the album of the month. Most times we weren't interested so we'd file our response, no thanks. Next thing you know we got the album of the month anyway and a bill for a fair sized amount. This went on for a couple of months and finally I got fed up.

The next time I got a bill from them both for me and Mitch, I never opened the envelope, but wrote on each one " Sorry, but Leslie Swartmann is deceased" and "Sorry, Mitch Klien is deceased". I never heard from Columbia records again. Had a good start to my record collection,though....

****

First I put an add in the Citizen looking for a roommate. There were 3 applicants, the first two were way too straight for me, I couldn't relate to them at all and figured no way could I live with these guys in close quarters. Number three was scary but interesting. Mathieu Gagne. He parked his 500 cc Bultaco motorcycle on the sidewalk beside the apartment building. He was loud, good looking, well dressed and articulate and though he was raised in a French home (his Dad was in the Military) he spoke perfect English.

I figured he's the one!

Chapter 12.

New Roomie...

It worked out well for the longest time. We became good friends and went clubbing together on his Bultaco. Our favourite spot at the time was the "Chaudeire" just after the Champlain Bridge on the way to Aylmer. Back then the favourite group was the "Staccatos" who later changed their name to the "Five Man Electric Band":

Mathieu was much more outspoken than me. He was loud, had a very engaging way about him, had a thunderous laugh. But while I liked his personality I wasn't impressed with his habits. When he took a bath, he left the tub dirty, never cleaned up the ring around the tub. If he ate something he never cleaned up his dish. When he changed his clothes, he heaved his dirty underwear into the corner of the bedroom. But he was entertaining.

One night the Jehovah Witnesses were canvassing our building. We usually left our apartment door open to create a breezeway in the summertime. Mathieu heard them coming down the hallway soliciting converts before they got to our door. I had no idea what was to follow.

I was laying in the tub soaking in hot water and soap when the Jehovah's got to our door. Mathieu invited them in. I thought, something wrong here, this guy is a devout Roman Catholic?

He was playing them. He had them churning out their best lines and he pretended he was taking it all in. Then they were all sitting around comfortably on the sofa and chair and all of a sudden, Mathieu fell off his chair onto his knees, threw his arms up in the air and started shouting in a very loud thunderous voice, like some Evangelist preacher in the US southwest Bible Belt: **"I BELIEVE!! I DO BELIEVE!!** Then thunderous laughter and again : **"I DO BELIEVE!! I SEE THE WAY!! GLORY BE TO GOD!!!"** then more thunderous laughter.

The Jehovahs at that point figured they had encountered a madman and left the apartment as fast as they could.

Meanwhile in the tub I'm thinking: *you crazy son of a bitch, what next?* chuckling away at the same time.

He matched it the very next week.

We had this paper boy who was about 11 or 12 years old. He had the whiniest, most grating tone of voice that just rubbed anyone the wrong way the minute he opened his mouth. He'd show up (always at suppertime) and announce in his full blown whiney voice: **"COLLECT FOR THE CITIZEN!!"**.

I guess Mathieu had been planning this for some time as he had closed the door and when the paperboy rapped on the door, he smiled at me and then scooted over to the door. He then bent down so his face would be at the same height as the paperboy. I thought to myself, Oh Oh, what's this all about?

Then Mathieu worked his face into a redfaced angry crazed look with eyes glassy and teeth snarling and sprang the door open and screamed at the unsuspecting paperboy: **"JUST HOW MUCH DO WE OWE YOU, BOY??"** Then came that hideous laughter of his. Sounded something you'd hear out of Vincent Price or Bela Lugosi… The paperboy ran away and never returned. We got a new paperboy the next week. Not whiney.

Chapter 14.

Then along came Ann.

There were four young girls that moved into a three bedroom apartment on the third floor. We were on the second floor and just happened to watch them the day they moved in with suitcases and clothes bags. We both offered to help them carry their stuff upstairs. They blushed and declined.

They were all from the same villages in Western Quebec: Chapeau, Waltham and Chichester. They were going to share their two bedroom apartment at $120 per month at $40 each or $10 per week. Back then, four girls could walk down the street to the corner IGA and get four huge bags of groceries for $20 bucks. This would last a week.

As I watched the four of them moving in I couldn't take my eyes off Ann. She was very small, about five feet tall, natural blonde hair, beautiful fair skin, penetrating blue eyes and very shy.

I thought to myself. "This is the one." It was love at first sight. But I was afraid to approach her too soon in case I blew it. Mathieu wasn't afraid. He asked her out and the next thing you know they were dating. I was not impressed.

He was not right for her. He was Mr. Big time City guy, loud, annoying, knew everything type person. He got Ann out on a first date. I think it didn't go that well. The next day he asked me what I thought of her. I said I think she's not your type, man. You need a very outgoing girl like yourself. She's a very shy country girl fresh in the city.

He said maybe you're right. I'm going to take her out on one more date, see if it works. I asked him where are you taking her?

He said : "I've got these two gay friends of mine. They're having a secret gay marriage in a hall up on Mountain Road above Aylmer on Friday night. It should be a blast. We'll go up in my Bultaco.

I guess the idea of going to a wedding in Aylmer Quebec on the back of Mathieu's Bultaco seemed exciting at first but when she got there and saw that most of the couples were gender equal whether male or female, she became uncomfortable.

Meanwhile, I was a regular customer of Hertz Rent A Car every weekend. I'd rented a Ford Galaxie 500 that weekend. It was parked on the street. I was crashed for the night and the phone rang at 1:00 o'clock in the morning. It was Ann. She was crying. She said:**" He brought me to this gay wedding! I didn't know. He's drunk now. He's gone somewhere. I'm scared Leslie!"**

I said: **"Don't be scared Ann, what's the name of the place you're at?"** She said : I don't know!! I said: **"Ask someone....** So she asked someone closeby and they said you're at St. Antoine's Parish Hall on Mountain Road.

I said:**" Hang tight, I'll be there in about a half an hour and bring you back home."**

She said: **"Oh thank you Leslie, please come soon....."**

I went downstairs two at a time jumped into the rent a car and peeled rubber on my way to Aylmer and the St. Antoine's Parish Hall.

It was early morning, no cars on the road, I made it to her in about 25 minutes from downtown Ottawa. When I got there she was standing outside the hall crying. I pulled up beside her and reached over and opened the door.

She jumped in and I said: **"We are out a here!!"** and hit the gas.

She stopped crying by the time we got to the Champlain Bridge and knew we were close to home.

I said: **"What ever possessed you to let that asshole take you to a Gay wedding?"**

She said: **" I had no idea, he said it was going to be a fun night when two of his friends were tying the knot…"**

Yeah right, I said. The conversation stopped there all the way back to the apartment. I parked outside, took her up to the third floor and walked her to her door.

I said: **"Here you are safe and sound. Better think twice before you go on any more rides on Mathieu's Bultaco."**

She put her key in the door, opened it and before she went in she hugged me and kissed me on the cheek and said: **"Thank you Leslie, You're my best friend!"**

I went back to my apartment being major depressed having been given a brotherly kiss by my major heart throb.

I don't know what time Mathieu rolled in that night but the next morning I wasn't too impressed with my roommate. After I made the morning coffee I woke him up. He was major hung over. I started to ask him what ever possessed him to take Ann to a deal like that and why did he abandon her?

He said:**" I don't know man, I drank too much then me and some guys smoked some weed and I passed out, man."**

Well isn't that just great, I said. Then I explained how I had to come and rescue her. He said: **"Hey man, my Bultaco's still up there… will you take me up there so I can bring it back home?"**

I said: **"Yeah right, kiss my arse!"**

He found a way to get his Bultaco back from Aylmer and announced the next day he was going on a "Fishing Weekend" with his Dad and their Army buddies. I said: "Fill your hat, man" (Popular expression back then).

Mathieu wasn't out the door five minutes and I was on the phone to Ann. I asked her: **"You got any plans tonight?"** She said: **"No, Why?"**

I said: **"Ever been to the Ottawa EX?"** She said: **"No, are you asking me on a date?"** I said boldly: **"Yes I am"**. Ann said: **"OK , Let's go… "**

She insisted that I bring along one of her roommates as well. When we got to the gate at the EX I paid her admission and mine and her roommate's. After we went through the turnstiles and started into the exhibition grounds I reached over and grabbed her hand. When I got the squeeze back I knew I was finally making headway.

We did the rounds, ate the hamburgers at the St.Andrew's Parish stand, ate the Candy floss and the Candy Apples. I won her a Teddy Bear at the milk bottle toss, and we went on some rides, I noticed she was hugging me closer on each ride.

We were finally played out and knew it was time to go home. We grabbed a bus on Bank Street that dropped us off right by our place. Ann was smiling all the way home. We went up to her door and this time I didn't get a brotherly hug and kiss on the cheek. She said: **" This was a great evening, Leslie, I loved it, Thank you… "**

Followed by a much warmer hug then a straight on the lips kiss.

I almost passed out right there. She said "Good Night, Leslie" and the door closed. I stood there for a few minutes mesmerized.

Then I went back to my apartment. That was it. She was the one. I knew it. I knew it before. Now I knew it for sure!

That weekend Mathieu returned from his "Fishing trip". I wasn't in a very good mood. I pointed out to him that I wasn't prepared to pick up his dirty clothes where he threw them on the floor and I wasn't too keen on cleaning up his dirty dishes after he had his late night snacks.

We agreed it was time to part company. He moved out and I was taking on the full rent. Then I decided I should charm Ann. She had mentioned her Dad was a great Country and Western Guitar Player.

She didn't know by then I either played the guitar or even that I could sing. By this time I had been through many guitars, but my latest was a Yamaha flattop that was modeled after a Martin. It was a nice machine.

I decided I'd practice my guitar and my songs with my apartment door open. Of course the folks on the third floor would hear me.

I knew what to do. She had told me her Dad was a big fan of Hank Williams, Sr., Hank Snow and Ernest Tubb.

Of course these were the songs I practiced. I would practice: "Your Cold Cold Heart" by Hank Williams. Then I'd do " Nobody's Child" by Hank Snow. Then I'd do "Walkin' the Floor Over you by Ernest Tubb". For good measure I'd throw in a Porter Wagoner Song: "Pick me up on your way down" just to seal the deal.

Ann and I started dating in earnest but I had a major problem with two former boyfreinds she was still clinging on to.

There was her childhood sweetheart back home. They dated all through High School and it was a generally accepted fact that these two would eventually marry. The other fellow in the equation was a remote cousin, very handsome and had dated her on occasion. There were pictures of both these men on her dresser.

Chapter 15.

That's it I've decided…

I started to show her all the sights and sounds of Ottawa. I took her to all the different restaurants: Chinese, Italian, Seafood, Steak Houses, that she really enjoyed. Then I took her to concerts. George Jones and Tammy Wynette were playing the Capitol Theatre. I got tickets. Harry Belafonte was playing the Arts Centre. I got tickets.

We used to frequent the Cathay House on Albert Street. The Manager got to know us very well and he called me Mister Leslie and Ann was Missus Leslie.

One night at the apartment we called in a take out order. I asked Ann to call it in and they owner said **" No problem, Missus Leslie!!"**

We were getting closer all the time. I went up to Peoples Credit Jewelers on Sparks Street. I was going to buy an engagement ring on layaway. The reason I fixed on this store was because they had been blasting the same jingle every year at Christmas time and it kind of sunk in your head. It went like this:

"Christmas comes but once a year and where will you go shopping"
Where will you go shopping?
Peoples Credit Jewelers, Peoples credit Jewelers.
The Home of Christmas Shopping!

**And what you'll buy for mother dear, father dear, brother dear
And where will you go shopping?
Where will you go shopping?
Peoples Credit Jewelers, People Credit Jewelers.
The home of Christmas Shopping!"**

I picked out a real nice ring it had 3 diamonds in it. It cost back then $400 which was a fortune but I went for it. I put it on layaway and went in sometimes twice a month to pay down my bill. I put a reserve on the matching Wedding ring.

Six months later it was paid in full. I picked up the small velvet box with that ring inside then I took it back home to my apartment and fretted for a few days. I'd open the box look at the ring. I'd say to myself, tomorrow I'll go and propose!

But I was chicken. She still had those pictures of the former boyfriends on her dresser and that intimidated me big time.

I decided she was going to have to make a choice so I went up and said: Ann, Why do you keep these pictures of those guys on your dresser all the time? Don't you realize the sight of them aggrevates me?

She said: **"OK Leslie, They don't mean anything to me anymore so I'll retire their pictures. I guess I should have put them away some time ago**

So the next night it was shit or get off the pot.

It was after suppertime. I said to myself, OK guy, this is it! Get your ass up there and do the deal.

I went up from the second floor to the third floor I rapped on Ann's door. Her roommate answered and invited me in.

Ann was in the kitchen doing dishes and said she'd be out in a minute.

I was very nervous. Finally she came out and said: **"What's up Leslie?"**

I said: **Would you sit down on the chair here as I have a very important question to ask you.**

She sat down and then I did the thing I was brought up to do. I kneeled down on my bended knee and said: **"Ann you know by now that I am very fond of you. In fact, I love you. I want to spend my whole life with you.**

Then I reached into my pocket and found the little ring box, opened it and said: **"I want to marry you Ann, I love you and want to put this engagement ring on your finger. Please say yes, Ann.**

Her eyes got shiny and she looked away from me. I got this terrible sinking feeling that I'd screwed up. Then she looked at me and smiled and said:" **I thought you'd never ask!"** I put the engagement ring on her finger and we kissed. Her roommates were smiling in the background.

This was the one of the happiest moments of my life. I finally found the girl of my dreams and she just agreed to marry me,. What could possibly go wrong?

We'll start with the parents and the parish priest.

Ann was 20. Back then you needed your parents consent and in the case of a Western Quebec catholic girl, the OK of the local parish priest!

The first hurdle was the parents. Her mom liked me right off the start. Her Dad was a different story. When Ann showed him the engagement ring he asked : **"So do you two have to get married? Is there a bun in the oven?"**

Ann said: **"Dad I love this guy, I'm not pregnant, Give him a break."**

Just then I noticed above the window in their mobile home Dad had both a fiddle and a mandolin.

As well he had a Gibson Guitar (a big one) and a Red Fender Mustang with a Marshall Amp. He was playing part-time on the weekends with a local band in hotels nearby.

Ann said: **"Daddy he may look like a City Slicker but when he picks up a guitar you'll realize he's a Country boy through and through.|**

He asked me if I knew any country songs. I said: **"Is the Pope Catholic?"** Ann smiled. I then did my version of "Hello Walls" by Faron Young.

He grabbed his Gibson and played lead runs behind my next song a Hank Williams Classic "You're Cheating Heart".

I had him from Hello Walls.

I passed the first test. Both Mom and Dad agreed that we could marry their daughter and gave their blessing. But I had to go and get approved by the local parish priest Father Raymond J Wilson.

He was a hard ass. He didn't like me at first. Here I was, coming up from Ottawa Big City guy taking his young parishioner girl who was supposed to marry her childhood sweetheart in his mind (and a lot of others). My heart was pounding in my chest and my hands were dripping with sweat.

He asked me: " **So what makes you think you're good enough to marry this girl?"**

"What do you do for a living? Can you support our Ann?"

I said **"I work as a commissioned collector at a Collection Agency in Ottawa. I make good money as I am one of the top collectors in the company."**

I then said: Sir, er, Father Wilson, I respect this girl, I love her and I'm very impressed how she attends Mass every Sunday. She's a much better Catholic than I am an Anglican.

"And what to you propose to do about that?" He said.

I think I'm going to turn Catholic I want my kids to grow up as devoted their church as their Mom,

Father Wilson said: **"You just said all the right things young man."**

He said I could go and everything would be just fine…

As I walked out of the office, I heaved a big sigh of relief. Back then young couples were encouraged to enroll in a "Marriage Course". We decided we'd do everything by the book. Besides, the wedding day wasn't going to happen anytime soon as I still had to pay off the matching wedding ring at Peoples Credit Jewellers.

Father Wilson called Ann's parents and asked them to get me to call him. I was in fear of how the conversation would go, but finally dialed his number.

He asked me if I was still serious about converting to the Roman Catholic Church. I said sure, I just didn't know how to get started. He informed that a good friend and fellow priest would be happy to give me my lessons and catechism. Upon completion I would be Baptized, Confirmed and accepted into the Church.

What he didn't tell me was his friend and fellow priest was the Auxiliary Bishop of Ottawa. The first interview was one night mid-week around 6:30 p.m. I had the pounding heart and sweaty hands all over again.

I was ushered into a very impressive office by the housekeeper. Moments later Rev. M.J. Woolam walked in. He had a typical priest's attire but had a red beanie on his head. Right off the bat I figured out he was a Bishop, and I started to freak out. But then the most amazing thing happened. He spoke. I never in my life heard anyone with such a soft, comforting and soothing voice in my entire life.

He said: **"You are Leslie, the young man that Father Raymond speaks so highly about"**.

This through me for an absolute loop as I didn't think I'd made all that favourable impression on the good Father Wilson.

Then the conversation flowed. It was so easy to talk to him. He was so.... Holy....

I figured this guy when he died would be an automatic Angel, no courses to take, automatic wings and a harp, soon as St. Peter lays eyes on him.

We set up a schedule of meetings and I would come at 7:00 p.m. Tuesdays and Thursdays. He mentioned that sometimes he wouldn't be able to personally be there but there was a retired priest from Fort Coulonge, Father Vachon, who would fill in for him when necessary.

I enjoyed our lessons. He was soft spoken but very engaging. He was impressed with my knowledge of the Old Testament and New Testament and how I could quote scriptures without the need of the Bible.

I explained to him that I'd read the Bible from cover to cover at least three times by the time I was fifteen. But I couldn't figure out Revelations and maybe I didn't want to.

The Anglican Church was a breakaway from the Roman Catholic Church in England under King Henry the Eight. He wanted to divorce his wife at the time but the Pope wouldn't grant his wish. So Henry the 8th decided he'd form his own church, appointed the Archbishop of Canterbury and got his divorce.

The new church was almost an exact duplicate of the Roman Catholic church with one small difference. It was founded and controlled by the King of England.

I asked Bishop Woolam how come in the Anglican's Apostles Creed it said : " I believe in the holy, catholic church, the communion of saints.…" He said Leslie, catholic means worldwide.

One day we digressed from the usual catechism work. We talked about his roots in Ashdad, Ontario (a small hamlet between Renfrew and Dacre.)

He asked me if I knew how Ashdad got it's name. I was a sucker for this one. He then explained that back in the old days a father and son had walked to Renfrew to get supplies. On the way back home the father said son, I need to rest. I'm going to sit for a while under the shade of this nice Oak tree.

The son replied: **"I think you're wrong Father, that's an Ash Dad!"**

Then Bishop Woolam busted out laughing and said : **"I got you good, eh Leslie?"**

I said yes sir you got me good.

It was now early April and the conversation went to my spring Brook Trout fishing. I explained that I'd been introduced to this creek in Nickabeau Quebec that was loaded with Brook Trout. I had been told by a local "Don't try to fish them until the dandelions turn white, Until then there's too much feed in the spring runoff."

I explained that the time was right and I was going for my annual snack of trout the next weekend. The Bishop said: "If you get any extras don't forget about your priest friend here in Ottawa, Leslie."

That weekend I scored bigtime. It seemed every time I threw in my line I ended up with a nice Brookie. I went two days in a row and caught way over my daily limit each day.

So I brought my catch home and took half of it for our feast and the other half (thirteen trout all about 6 inches long) cleaned them, salted them, wrapped them in Waxed paper and froze them.

The following Tuesday night I showed up with a cooler for my lessons. The Bishop asked me: **"What's in that cooler, Leslie?"** I said: **" A snack of Nickabeau Brook Trout!!"**

He and the other priests and the Housekeeper had a feast the following night with brook trout fried in flour and butter and enjoyed every bite.

Things progressed well. I was to be baptized and confirmed before June. We had set our Wedding date for early August.

My best friend at the time Ritchie enlisted his brother and wife to be my Godfather and Godmother. I was baptized in June and confirmed in July.

Then came August.

Meanwhile the old boyfriend (Childhood sweetheart) was being a pest. He was coming around Ann's place on the weekends and telling her parents I wasn't right for her and then telling her the same thing when she was up on a weekend visiting her parents.

Her Dad was the one who put the whole thing to rest. He told her, make up your mind. Are you going to marry this guy or not? Tell the former flame to get off your case and get lost!

After that things went well.

The wedding day arrived. My Mom and Dad were there and very pleased. The wedding was scheduled for 11:00 a.m. We were all gathered at the church and awaiting the arrival of the bride to be. All my groomsmen were there except one. He was my boss from the Ottawa Collection Agency and had got pretty plastered after our wedding rehearsal the night before.

Finally Ann and her Dad pulled up. Still missing groomsman #3. He was staying at a hotel in Pembroke and didn't hear his wake up call. They played "Here comes the Bride" then stopped when they realized there wasn't a full Bridal party. Somebody ran next door to the church and recruited a friend of the family, our age to stand in for the late groomsman.

Dan arrived soon in a green suit with a red tie and running shoes. It wasn't a matching tux, but we didn't care. The Service proceeded. Bishop Woolam had came up from Ottawa to officiate with Father Wilson. Another priest from the parish stood in as well. So after I said to Ann, **"Looks like we've been triple married"**

We had our Wedding pictures taken by a professional photographer from Pembroke. We couldn't really afford it, but he made arrangements for us to finance it through TCC (Trans Canada Credit).

Then came the reception. We had our going away outfits on, Ann having shedded her Wedding Dress and I'd shedded my tux.

We went down to the reception hall which I thought would be a few people, family members, some friends. I wasn't prepared for what was to happen after the Dinner.

In a sideroom besides the Bar and reception area there was a table loaded with wedding gifts. There was toasters, dishes, knives and fork sets, all kinds of kitchen utensils. Then we had our Dinner.

Barb's Parish Priest was the first speaker. He got up and said a few words and blessed our marriage. Her Dad who was a very reserved person said a few words that basically said he and Ann's Mom were welcoming me to the family. My Best man Michael was the next one up. He read from a prepared text that got a lot of laughs and embarrassed me. Ann's cousin Elwood was the last to get up and his speech was short and sweet. He said: **"Enough talk, now let's get down to some serious drinking!!"**

What really blew me away was after the dinner when the reception started it seemed that everyone in the community rolled in. Every time I turned around someone was stuffing a one or two dollar bill in my or Ann's hand and saying:Congratulations! Ann's Dad was a very popular performer in a local country and western band and was well liked in the community.

While everyone was stuffing one and two dollar bills in my hand I had a major shock from Bishop Woolam. He handed me an envelope and said: **"Put this in your pocket Leslie, but don't ever tell anyone what's inside, is that a promise?"**

"Yes Sir" : I said.

It turned out there was a twenty dollar bill in the envelope.

By the time the night was over we had about $400 dollars for our honeymoon. (Back then $400 was like a small fortune!)

We left about ten p.m. after loading all the presents in our car as we were going to Ottawa to spend our first night in our new apartment before taking off on our honeymoon.

Chapter 16.
The Honeymoon

The next morning we got up early. We were going to Montreal to see EXPO 67, one year later. We stopped in Hawkesbury and had a nice breakfast at a roadside diner, then proceeded on to Montreal. When we got well into Montreal we had to get off the Metropolitan Freeway for gas. The owner of the gas station asked us where we were going. We said we were on our honeymoon and we wanted to see EXPO 67 sight and the Shrine of St. Andre.

He asked where we were going to stay that night. We said we were looking for a nice hotel.

He said in broken English: " Dem Hotels dey soak yer money. You doan need dat. You get nice Bed an' Brekfass!" I Got juss da spot for you, Cheep!"

He made a phone call and very soon a car showed up that would guide us to our destination. We decided we'd go and see what was the deal.

A few blocks later we pulled into a very nice older residential district. There was an elderly couple waiting for us at the front door of their house. They were very friendly and told us we could stay there for B & B for $30.

We decided we'd go for it because by then we were both exhausted. They escorted us to our room which was a nice very small bedroom with twin beds. The husband said: **"Is it true, you are on your honeymoon?"**

Then he said to his wife: **"Carmen, we have to pull those twin beds together!"**

We said, No No No. but they insisted.

Then we brought in our luggage and settled down.

After we were settled in, there was a knock on the door.

"We have a small treat for the newlyweds!!" They said. We opened the door and the old couple were standing there with big grins on their faces. They handed me two glasses, a bottle of wine and a plate of chocolate chip cookies. And said: **"Goodnight young Mr. and Mrs.!!"**

The next day we left after thanking that wonderful old couple and found our way to the Shrine of St.Andre. Ann had heard about it from her Aunt and wanted to see it firsthand. When we got there we saw we had this incredible amount of stairs to climb. But we did it. And we saw it, Ann bought a medallion and a souvenir and we left on the next stop.

We toured the sight of EXPO 67 then made our way out of Montreal. Our final destination on our Honeymoon was to be Lake Placid, New York.

At Lake Placid there was an animal farm, Whiteface Mountain and the North Pole amusement park. We saw it all and on our way back to the motel I stopped at a roadside stand to get some frozen custard.

I asked Ann if she would like a frozen custard and she declined. I went to the stand and ordered mine then I thought I should get one for Ann, anyway.

When I got back to the car I handed her her cone and she broke out in tears and cried: **"I didn't want the damned cone!"**

I was devasted. I pitched her cone into the nearest garbage can and we headed back to the motel.

It was then that I finally got my first modicum of smarts about women. It's a constant learning process, but I've been working on it ever since.

Before we got to the motel I said: **"Ann maybe it's time to get back home. We've had a good time up until now, but maybe we're both homesick for Canada, and I think we should get home and open up our wedding presents. What do you think?"**

She smiled and said: **"Oh Leslie, you read my mind!"**

I guess she's been training me ever since.

Next year we'll celebrate our 41st Anniversary.

As I always tell her:, **"I couldn't have picked a better wife out of the Simpson's Sears Catalogue!"**

That always makes her smile.

The End.